D0439127

Your Quest for God

Richard A. Bennett

Published by:
CROSS CURRENTS
INTERNATIONAL MINISTRIES
P.O. Box 1058
Lynden, WA 98264

www.ccim-media.com/resources

Printed in the United States of America

Library of Congress Catalog Card Number: 98-67799

ISBN: 1-57736-114-8

Paragraphs two and three, pages 33 from Evidence that Demands a Verdict by
Josh McDowell, © 1972, 1979. Published by Here's Life Publishers. Used by
permission.

Unless otherwise noted Scripture quotations are from *The New American
Standard Bible* -- The Lockman Foundation 1960, 1962,1963,1968, 1971,
1972,1973,1975,1977. Used by permission. Bold print with Scripture
quotations are added by the author.

Scripture quotations marked NIV are from *The Holy Bible, New International
Version* -- 1973, 1978, 1984, International Bible Society. Used by permission.

Scripture quotations marked NS are from *The New Schofield Reference Bible,
King James Version* -- 1967 by Oxford University Press, Inc. Reprinted by
permission.

Scripture quotations marked Amp are from The Amplified New Testament --
The Lockman Foundation 1954, 1958. Used by permission.

Scripture quotations marked NKJV are from *The New King James Vesion-
New Testament* -- 1979, 1982, Thomas Nelson, Inc., Publishers. Used by
permission.

Scripture quotations marked KJ are from *The King James Version. All scriptures
are in italics*. Emphases by author.

"Distributed without charge by:
HOPE FOR TODAY MINISTRIES
Donations used towards reprinting
further copies through an **HFT** available
"designated fund."

HFT publications
PO Box 3927 • Tustin, CA 92781
1-800-75-BIBLE
In Canada (604) 851-5436

Without the encouragement, the love,
the sacrifice and the prayers
of my wife, Dorothy,
this book would not have been written.
As Paul said of Phoebe, so I say of her: . .
She herself has also been a helper
of many . . . and of myself as well.

Contents

Foreword

I heartily recommend this book, *Your Quest for God,* for two reasons. The first is that I know the author! He is a son in the faith, and I have no greater joy than to hear that my children walk in truth (3 John 4 KJ).

The second reason is more objective. Dr Richard Bennett has done a superb job in spelling out clearly, concisely and convincingly the essentials of man's relationship with God.

The Bible informs us that God has *set eternity in the hearts of men . . . (Ecclesiastes 3:11 NIV).* It follows, therefore, that since men were made for eternity the things of time can never fully and permanently satisfy. There is an endless emptiness which only God can fill. St. Augustine stated it perfectly when he declared, "O God, Thou hast made us for Thyself, and our souls are restless till they rest in Thee." This book helps us to follow that quest until we find rest in a living and personal relationship with the Eternal God.

It is my earnest prayer that multitudes will read the pages that follow and heed the message that unfolds to the glory of God and their eternal good.

Dr. Stephen F. Olford

Preface

*I*n our extensive travels, my wife, Dorothy, and I have met many friends on the highways and byways of life. They have come from many different cultures, economic backgrounds and educational levels.

We do not believe it was by accident that we met these individuals. Neither do we believe it is accidental that this little book is in your hands.

Over the years, the most important conversations we have had with our many friends have centered around our quest for God. Some of the thoughts we have shared together are contained in this book.

The first edition of *Your Quest for God*, from which the subsequent revisions were made, was a personal project of thanksgiving. As Dorothy and I approached our 25th wedding anniversary, we pondered what would be the most vital way we could express our thanks to God for His goodness to us.

What better way, we thought, than by writing, printing and giving to 25,000 people a message that would bring them hope and peace. That would be one thousand for each year of our married life.

God blessed this little labor of love as the book literally found its way around the world. All 25,000 copies were placed directly into the hands of people in many different countries. Our greatest joy was to receive letters from those who, as a result of reading *Your Quest for God,* found new purpose in life.

Numerous requests came that we translate this book into other languages. Therefore, we decided to make the first revision of the text for this purpose with the prayer that many more people throughout the continents of the world would be helped in their 'Quest for God.' As a result, over three million copies in fifty languages have been printed and distributed far and wide. And now we also pray that this fifth English edition will bring help to even more readers.

The first two chapters will not be equally relevant to every reader. Chapter one was written for those people who may question the existence of God. Although chapter two will be of particular interest to those who have learned to question everything, it is actually vital to all readers, for it encourages each of you to evaluate your own beliefs and attitudes.

These preparatory chapters, however, are essential to the overall theme, for they help establish the trustworthiness of the remaining information. Chapters three to ten contain basic truths that will help you in your quest for God. So, we gladly place this new edition in the hands of God to bless as He deems best.

Both Dorothy and I wish to record our thankfulness to God for the love, prayers and insights of the many special people who have shared their personal experience of God with us. They are far too many to name. To these friends we say: "Thank you."

Richard A. Bennett

Geology is the autobiography of the earth but, like all autobiographies, it does not go back to the beginning.

Sir Charles Lyell

Chapter 1

Is there really a God?

There may have been times in your life when things seemed so bleak that you have not only doubted the love of God but you have also questioned His very existence.

In the Bible, the existence of God is not explained; neither is it proved. It is simply taken for granted. The very first sentence of the Bible *In the beginning God created the heavens and the earth (Genesis 1:1)* is an awesome statement that is both simple and profound. It declares that God is, and that He is the Creator of the Universe.

Many years ago my wife held a senior nursing position at one of the most prestigious psychiatric hospitals in Europe. One day a leading psychiatrist, who claimed to be an atheist, quizzed Dorothy about her faith. "Doctor," she replied, "you know I respect you very deeply as an authority in your field. You are an esteemed university lecturer, and in the medical profession your name is widely revered. May I suggest, however, that before you again claim to be an atheist, you read the Bible with the same zeal that has characterized your psychiatric research."

She then reminded him of several of his patients who had recently been released from the chronic ward because of the wonderful changes God's power had made in their lives. She was able to name one or two who had been so dramatically transformed that they were already leading productive lives. Dorothy told the renowned psychiatrist how each of these patients had come to know God in a personal and vital way. The doctor himself was acutely aware that these patients had been previously untouched by the latest psychiatric techniques. Neither as an atheist, nor even as a psychiatrist, could he account for the phenomenon of their changed lives.

This doctor, having just told Dorothy that he did not believe in God, concluded that conversation by asking her to pray for him! He also promised that, for the first time in his life, he would start to read the Bible with an open mind.

After seven weeks of careful reading, the psychiatrist told Dorothy that he was no longer a professing atheist. However, he still had a problem, for he recognized that a genuine commitment to God would require a change in his lifestyle. "My problem is no longer intellectual," he admitted, "but I find that I am unwilling to accept the changes that would occur if I were to become a committed believer."

After having prayed for our doctor friend for ten years, we finally received a letter in which he told us of his new-found faith and of his personal commit-ment to God. We were overjoyed, but not too surprised, because we knew that *faith cometh by hearing, and hearing by the Word of God (Romans 10:17 KJ).*

To help each of us come to know Him, God has placed within our being a deep inner consciousness of His existence.

Some people may choose not to believe in God, but there has never been a person on Planet Earth who could not believe in God.

Even in the physical universe itself, God has given many evidences of His own existence. The deeper that our twenty-first century science reaches into the secrets of the universe, the more unreasonable it becomes to suggest that all this came into existence without a Designer. No one would ever suggest that a space shuttle could soar into space, orbit the Earth, and then land at the expected moment and location without the combined creative genius of designers, technicians and mathematicians. Likewise, sunsets and seasons, galaxies and atoms, the force of gravity and the power of love could never exist without the planning and design of a Creator God.

Surely it takes a million times more faith to believe that an ordered, perfect Creation came from a 'big bang' than it does to believe in God, the Creator, for there can be no design without first there being a designer.

Even the government that has denied the existence of God has actually expressed its own confidence in the universe's being one of law and order each time that it has sent a cosmonaut into space. Only by cooperating with these laws could their cosmonauts have returned safely to earth. Does it not seem strange, then, that these same people who rely on natural laws reject the existence of a Lawmaker, the existence of a Supreme Planner?

Again we are all aware of the devastatingly-destructive power that is released when an atom bomb explodes. However, it has been calculated that each and every second the sun releases an amount of power that is equal to 5,000 billion atomic bombs. And in comparison to the other power-emitting stars, our sun is not even very large; and we still do not know how many stars there actually are in the universe. Although billions have been gathered into man's sight, these stars could be just the outer fringe of the vast unknown. Today, though, astronomers recognize that the energy released in some galaxies is billions of times greater than that given off by our own sun! How could such power exist were it not for a Creator whose power is without limit?

Indeed, creation introduces us to a God of Design, a God of Law and a God of Infinite Power. The Bible says:

> *The heavens declare the glory of God; and the firmament showeth His handiwork. Day unto day uttereth speech, and night unto night showeth knowledge. There is no speech nor language, where their voice is not heard. Their line is gone out through all the earth, and their words to the end of the world (Psalm 19:1-4 KJ).*

For the invisible things of Him [God] from the creation of the world are clearly seen, being understood by the things that are made, even His eternal power and Godhead; so that they are without excuse (Romans 1:20 KJ).

So, there is no excuse for anyone, anywhere, to deny the existence of God.

Reflecting upon the vastness, the order and the power that God has created makes many people feel very small and insignificant.

Israel's King David had that reaction and expressed it this way:

When I consider Thy heavens, the work of Thy fingers, the moon and the stars, which Thou hast ordained; what is man, that Thou dost take thought of him? (Psalm 8:3,4).

Today, our knowledge of the starry heavens has become vastly increased, for giant telescopes magnify our vision of the universe by half-a-million-fold and satellites signal pictures back to Planet Earth as they journey through outer space. As a result, we too might be tempted to ask the same question as did David: "How could a God who created all this be interested in little me?"

Fortunately, however, the age of the telescope is also the age of the microscope. Today, we know that there is also a world in miniature, which can be seen only through the microscope, and it is just as incredible as is the vastness of outer space. Even light is too coarse to reveal the secrets of this sub-microscopic realm. What escapes the eye of the scientist's traditional lab microscope can be picked up by the electron microscope, which further reveals the beauty, design, law and power embodied in our infinitesimally-minute world.

So, if you ever wonder whether or not God has someone so small as you on His mind, listen to the nuclear physicist tell how important real smallness is to the preservation of the entire universe. Separate the neutrons and the protons of an atom by just 1/12 trillionth of an inch and, instead of matter being bound in a solid mass, the world would blow apart in a cosmic nuclear explosion. Yes, smallness is just as important as greatness to the God of Creation.

It is reassuring to know that when we ask the question: *What is man that Thou dost take thought of him?* it is not the size of a man that determines his value. On the contrary, our personal value to God is predicated upon some very different factors. And God has revealed to us why we are valuable to Him and how precious we are in His sight.

Though creation itself speaks of a God of design, law and power, God has chosen another way to reveal Himself as the God of infinite love and mercy, the One who desires nothing but our greatest good. But if you are to find such a God, it is imperative that your spiritual guide be utterly reliable.

Pause to Consider

1. If you threw a handful of iron filings into the air, would you expect to catch a Swiss watch when it came down?

2. Could the universe with all of its marvellous and intricate design have just happened without the Creator-God?

3. Though creation can point you to a Creator-God who has manifested Himself as the God of design, of law and of power, is creation of and by itself sufficient to bring you to an understanding of God's love and mercy?

A dark cave can easily be traversed by one who has entered it with a torch.

PLATO

Nature is the dim light from the cave's mouth; the torch is Scripture.

A.H. STRONG

Chapter 2

Is your spiritual guide reliable?

*S*ome time ago newspapers recounted the alarming fact that the tragic loss of human life in an airplane crash had been caused by a faulty radar signal. And yet that tragic accident pales into insignificance when compared to what happens if people put their confidence in a 'spiritual radar system' which directs them to spiritual disaster.

Today there are many conflicting and confusing voices in the world, each claiming to be a guide to God. How can you know which one to trust? In your quest for God you cannot afford to be guided by the wrong voice because the issues at stake are eternal.

British Prime Minister W. E. Gladstone wrote: "The Bible is stamped with a speciality of origin, and an immeasurable distance separates it from all its competitors."

American President Abraham Lincoln once said: "I believe the Bible is the best gift God has ever given to man."

Even though many great men of history have indeed testified to its uniqueness, the Bible really stands on its own record.

King David was clear about the reliability of his spiritual guide. He said: *Thy word is a lamp to my feet, and a light to my path (Psalm 119:105).*

To this very day people are finding the Bible can be trusted to guide them to God. In spite of those who have tried to destroy its credibility, the Bible stands as firm and faithful today as it did in days gone by; it is truly unique among the writings of the world.

Because people need the assurance that the Bible is both unique and authentic, God has stamped it with many seals that verify its being 'The Word of God.' Both within the pages of Scripture and also from the records of secular history, an honest enquirer will find overwhelming evidence to support the fact that: *All Scripture is inspired by God (2 Timothy 3:16).*

If the Bible had been written by one writer, we would not be surprised to find its theme developing in an orderly and progressive manner. This Book of Books, however, was not written by one person, but by many different authors from diverse cultures over a time span of several centuries; yet it contains a consistent, orderly and unique development of the truth about God. That in itself is most remarkable, more than remarkable—miraculous!

In addition, archaeological diggers are continually unearthing new evidence which further confirms the historical accuracy of the Bible record. Events that were once ridiculed as fiction have now been verified by the spades of modern archaeologists.*

Yes, the Bible truly is God's Book containing God's message to all people.

In spite of the fact that the Bible is God's Book, some people are still 'turned off ' from reading it because of a popular delusion that the world is divided into two groups: scientists who face the facts, and true believers who shut their eyes to them. The implication is that a real scientist cannot be a true believer. Today, however, there are many great scientists who deny this assumption. Though the Bible is not a scientific textbook, wherever it does touch on these areas it has never been discredited by established scientific facts. Instead, in its purpose and design, the Bible goes far beyond the limitations of science.

For instance, science cannot explain why we are here on Planet Earth, nor can it tell us where we are going after our life here on earth ends. Neither can science tell us what life is all about, or even the real value of a person. No matter how clever (or simple) a person may be, each one needs divine help to come to know

---

* For example, in 1868, a German traveller named Klein visited the ancient land of Moab, which is today called 'Jordan.' There he discovered a stone monument on which were inscribed thirty-four lines written by Mesha, King of Moab. This inscription was recorded in memory of his revolt against Israel. Both Omri and Ahab are mentioned in II Kings 1 and again on the monument. In both cases we are told that these Israelite kings were oppressors of Moab. Many such modernday discoveries confirm the historical accuracy of the Biblical record.

the truth about God. That is surely why the French philosopher and mathematician, Blaise Pascal, said: "The supreme achievement of reason is to show us that there is a limitation to reason." We would never have reliable answers to life's most important questions if it were not for God's Book.

Now let us consider two strong indications that the Bible is in fact God's Book.

The first is the incredible accuracy of its prophetic predictions. The second is the powerful and positive influence that it has exerted in the lives of those people who have taken its message seriously.

The Bible's Prophetic Accuracy

There is a built-in curiosity in most of us to know what the future holds. And the Bible reveals some of the most important events of the future, many in intricate and fascinating detail. Now you may well ask: "How can you be so sure?"

To answer this question let us imagine that you are taking a walking holiday in a country where you have never been before. The map in your hand is your only guide. Yesterday you found this map to be totally reliable for, just as it had indicated, you had found a river and then the village where you slept last night. Today you must decide a new path to take. Before you is unfamiliar territory, but your map indicates that if you turn left you will go through some woods to a place where you will find a large lake. Now you would like to see that lake, so what would you do? I think you would follow the directions of the map and take a left turn. Surely, the main reason for your confidence in doing this would be the fact that yesterday your map proved to be an accurate guide in an unknown territory. It told you what you would find before you got there, and it was right!

One of the most remarkable proofs that the Bible is the Word of God is its unique accuracy when it prophesies future events. In its pages we read many prophecies which, from today's perspective, we know have been exactly fulfilled even as they had been predicted hundreds of years before.

These prophecies cover a remarkable scope, embracing all the peoples of the earth, as well as including very specific details about Israel and the Middle East. Even more important are the hundreds of predictions relating to the coming of the Messiah. Because many of these messianic prophecies are now history, we recognize how incredibly accurate they were in some extremely unlikely details about the Messiah's birth, life and death.

On the basis of such a track record, it is reasonable (and right) to assume that the future will unfold exactly as the Bible predicts. And each year, further evidence of the Bible's prophetic accuracy unfolds before our very eyes. In fact, to read the Bible is to read tomorrow's newspaper.

Dr. Wilbur Smith was a life-long student of the Bible. He took particular delight in pointing out the detailed accuracy of Bible prophecy. Contrasting the many prophecies in the Old Testament that speak of the

Messiah with the teachings of others who claim to have the truth, Wilbur Smith noted that "Mohammedanism cannot point to any prophecies of the coming Mohammed uttered hundreds of years before his birth. Neither can the founders of any cult rightly identify any ancient text which specifically foretells their appearance."

Now we must acknowledge that there are certain so-called 'prophecies' which do not require much inspiration to be accurate.

With the aid of computers, election-day interviews and historical data, the news media can sometimes predict the winner of an election before the ballot boxes close. With all the statistics that are available to them, there is nothing very remarkable when they 'call' the winner ahead of time, and even then they sometimes miss!

However, try asking any news reporter to identify the candidates who will be running for election twenty or fifty years from now. Ask him who will win, and then ask him for details about the places where the winners will be born, their future lifestyles, and even the circumstances that will surround their deaths. Go even beyond that and ask the news reporter for reliable information about what will happen in the Middle East 1,000 years from now. Also ask him to specify cities that will be annihilated during that long period of time.

Surely you will agree that each time an additional prediction is demanded of that news reporter the incredible odds against his being accurate in his prophecy are vastly increased. That is, of course, unless the

God of eternity were telling him about the future; only in that case would we expect the reporter to know the end from the beginning. And such occurrences as those we have suggested for our news reporter together with many of even more intricate detail and covering an even longer time span have been prophesied in the Bible.

The history of the city of ancient Tyre, for example, is an incredible fulfillment of what God predicted would happen to this city.

If you are so inclined, first read the prophecies that are recorded in Ezekiel 26, verses 3-21, and then turn to the *Encyclopedia Britannica* and other records of history. In both you will be reading the same story, the first one as prophecy, and the second one as history.

Prophecy: A long time before the events occurred, God prophesied a turbulent future for the city of Tyre. He said:

> *Behold, I . . . will bring up many nations against you, . . . they will destroy the walls of Tyre and break down her towers.* Also, it was foretold that the very site on which this city of fame was built would be scraped to *make her a bare rock.* Even more than that, it was prophesied that they will . . . *throw your stones and your timbers and your debris into the water.* But the incredible details of these prophecies do not conclude with that. God said of ancient Tyre: . . . *you will be a place for the spreading of nets (Ezekiel 26:3,4,12,14).*

History: When you read the historical records, you will verify that when Nebuchad-nezzar destroyed the old (mainland) city of Tyre, he did indeed break down the walls and towers just as had been predicted. And later the engineers of Alexander the Great did scrape the ancient city of Tyre clean and did leave her like *a bare rock.*

When they threw the rubble of the city into the sea to make a causeway to the island, it was just as it had been prophesied: the stones and the timber and the dust were in fact thrown *into the water.* Yes, to this very day the ruins of ancient Tyre are buried by the waters of the sea. God said it would happen and it did.

Though there is a well-known city called Tyre in the Middle East today, this is not the ancient city of Tyre which was finally destroyed in 1291.

If you were able to visit the site of ancient Tyre, you would see an even more incredible fulfillment of these prophecies. There you would view a few fishermen's cottages clustered together in a little village, where you would view fishing boats drifting out to sea and fishing nets drying on bare rocks! How could human wisdom have predicted this unlikely future for such a thriving commercial city as that of ancient Tyre?

Peter Stoner compared seven prophecies about Ancient Tyre with the historical record. After calculating the mathematical probability that Ezekiel's prophecies would be fulfilled, he stated:

"If Ezekiel had looked at Tyre in his day, and made these seven predictions in human wisdom, these estimates mean that there would have been one chance in 75,000,000 of their all coming true. They all came true in the minutest detail."

Now let us look at just one of the predictions concerning the birth of a baby.

Matthew, a retired government tax official, recalled four of the many remarkable prophecies that were fulfilled when Jesus was born. In one of them, Matthew referred to the prophet Micah, who had thundered denunciations against the phony rulers of his day. Micah's heart was broken because when he was alive his nation lacked genuine leadership authority. However, Micah saw a brighter future when God showed him that one day a Ruler would be born. He even pinpointed the exact birthplace of this coming Leader.

> *But as for you, Bethlehem Ephrathah, too little to be among the clans of Judah, from you One will go forth for Me to be **ruler** in Israel. His goings forth are from long ago, from the days of eternity (Micah 5:2).*

God revealed that the needed Ruler in Israel would be born in Bethlehem Ephrathah.

Just as Micah prophesied, Jesus was born, not in His family's home town of Nazareth, but in Bethlehem Ephrathah; born there because of the decree of a Roman Emperor. It was census time and His parents were obeying an imperial decree. Accordingly, they left home to go to Bethlehem. Surely no one would look for the Ruler from little Bethlehem, which was only one of many Judean towns. The odds against His being born there are incredible. Yet it happened just as Micah had predicted. And this is only one of literally hundreds of such amazing prophecies about the life of Jesus.

We read that God declares:

The end from the beginning and from ancient times things which have not been done, saying, 'My purpose will be established and I will accomplish all My good pleasure' (Isaiah 46:10).

I declared the former things long ago and they went forth from My mouth, and I proclaimed them. Suddenly I acted, and they came to pass. . . . Therefore I declared them to you long ago, before they took place I proclaimed them to you (Isaiah 48:3,5).

History has proved that these prophecies, given by God and recorded in the Bible, have a 100% accuracy rating.

The Bible's Powerful Influence

A second powerful proof that the Bible is the Word of God is the influence that it has exerted. Socially, culturally and individually the message of the Bible has dignified the human race whenever and wherever it has been taught and believed.

Just before the first revision of this book was to go to print, a new friend visited our home. Together we reviewed the manuscript. Though not readily given to a display of emotion, he became quite overcome with tears as we read Chapter Seven. Twice we stopped to bow in prayer and to give praise to the God whose love we were reading about. Together we thanked God for His patience, His mercy and for every token of His love in our unworthy lives. As we sensed the vibrant, vital presence of the living God, we were filled with joy.

That day was especially significant for my friend. Exactly one year earlier, he had been sitting alone in a luxury apartment which was quite a contrast to the modesty of the dwelling where we now met.

But at that time the beauty that had surrounded him had given him no joy. In fact, he had such inward despair that he had no real desire to live. In his quest for personal happiness, he had indulged all the animal impulses of his manhood. A cocaine habit had cost him a fortune. 'Downers' and 'uppers', brandy and whisky all had been part of his daily drag. For years, in Europe and around the world, he had partied with the wealthiest of the wealthy, but on that night he was alone. In his solitude, his memory-induced despondency was now deepened by what he considered to be a threatening and fearful world situation. For him there seemed no way out.

With grim determination he loaded his twin-barreled handgun, held it to his temple and cocked the trigger. "Just 1/8 of an inch away from oblivion," he thought, "then my pain will be over forever." At that split second (my friend does not know how it happened) the television program changed. He found himself listening to a message from the Bible that presented a future of hope. As the midnight hour approached and quite alone, he fell on the floor before the living God to ask for forgiveness and mercy.

Because the power of God had so radically transformed my friend's life, the man before me bore little resemblance to the one I have briefly described. Before his birth, his parents had prayed for him; and though as a young man he had studied the Bible, he had refused to take its message seriously. In his world of affluence and privilege, he had rebelled against God and indulged in incredible moral license.

Seventeen years before that memorable night when he eventually found God, my friend had bought a beautiful leather-bound book. It contained blank white pages. His intent had been to record every significant event of his life from that day on. And yet nothing in those seventeen years of extravagant and wasteful living had merited one entry.

The fact is that all during those years my friend, having turned his back upon the living God, had traveled a strange and unsatisfying pseudo-spiritual journey. It had begun with an interest in the daily horoscope and an obsession with rock music and rock concerts. Soon he became involved in the occult. Later his fascination with Yoga led to a serious study of Hindu philosophy and to eventual involvement with Eastern Mysticism. Nothing that he had experienced during those years had merited a single entry in his brown leather notebook. Its pages remained white with the ache of emptiness until that memorable night when he met God.

That night my friend recorded his first entry. I had the joy of reading what he wrote. It is a sacred and spiritual account of a needy man who was saved by a loving God. It is beautiful indeed. In great mercy, God had broken through his spiritual blindness and had delivered him from despair and death by the light of His unchanging truth and amazing love.

It is because of man's spiritual confusion like the blindness of my friend that God has revealed Himself in a book that is called the Bible. If you turn **from** the Bible, the only reliable spiritual guide, you will shut yourself up in delusion and error. But if, in your search for God, you turn **to** the Bible with a teachable mind, you will find it to contain all the spiritual light and direction that you need.

Only through God's Word can we gain a clear understanding of God as He has declared Himself. In this Book, we are introduced to Truth itself, to the Word of God, to the Light of the World.

> Lord, Thy Word abideth,
> And our footsteps guideth;
> Who its truth believeth,
> Light and joy receiveth.

Pause to Consider

1. Are there any other manuscripts or 'sacred writings' that can compare with the Bible in their accuracy in predicting future events?

2. Do you personally know people whose lives have been transformed because they have heeded the message of the Bible?

3. Have you ever belittled the unique teachings of the Bible while at the same time you neglected to read it with an open mind?

*The problems of heaven and earth,
though they were to confront us together
and at once, would be nothing compared
with the overwhelming problem of God:
that He is; what He is like; and what we
as moral beings must do about him.*

A.W. TOZER

Chapter 3

What is God like?

At some time in life most people have asked: "What is God like?" Though God has given an answer to this question, there are still those who would rather rely on their imagination and speculation than read in the Bible what God has to say about Himself.

These people really reverse an important Bible statement. Whereas God said: *Let Us make man in Our image (Genesis 1:26),* they say: "Let us make God in our image." And so they change the *glory of the incorruptible God into an image made like corruptible man (Romans 1:23 NKJV).* Every 'god' that has been conceived by man has been totally powerless, and sometimes even grotesque.

No matter how clever a person is, he can never discover the living God by worldly wisdom . . . *the world through its wisdom did not come to know God (1 Corinthians 1:21).* If God could be discovered by human cleverness, He would be too small to be God. Not only that, but if human cleverness were necessary to discover God, then those people who may not be quite so clever would be disadvantaged in their quest for Him. And that is not the case.

On the contrary, spiritual wisdom is available to everybody. It is equally as available to an African 'stick lady' as it is to a university professor, for spiritual wisdom is not acquired by the academic process. It is available to all people who are humble enough to recognize their need of God's help in their quest for Him.

> *But if any of you lacks wisdom, let him ask of God, who gives to all men generously (James 1:5).* This kind of wisdom is not worldly but Heavenly. It is the *wisdom which none of the rulers of this age* (i.e., rulers who operate by this world's system) *has understood . . . not the spirit of the world, but the Spirit who is from God, that we might know the things freely given to us by God (1 Corinthians 2:8,12).*

The Bible is not merely a religious thesis; it is primarily the record of how God has revealed Himself to man. And only God can give you the spiritual wisdom that you need to understand who He is and what He wants to do in your life.

If you but ask Him, God will show Himself to you through His Holy Word.

In our travels we have found deep spiritual interest and insights in what some might consider unusual places and among unlikely people. For instance, one day we met a group of young African boys in the bush of Kenya who seemed interested only in sharing their faith and learning more about the things of God.

The equatorial sun had quickly slipped below the

horizon, bringing an end to a long, busy day. As I sat on a rock beside a dusty Kenyan lane to rest awhile, I heard a movement in the bush. I turned to see a faint ray from the full moon as it reflected in the large black eyes of an African boy. Soon this 10-year-old lad was squatting beside me on the rock; we quickly became good friends. Other boys heard our voices and seemed to come from nowhere to hear what we were talking about. Their knowledge of the Bible impressed me greatly.

"Why didn't God let Moses see His face?" my little friend asked.

Fascinated by such a question, I responded by asking young Joel if he could remember the prayer of Moses before God said to him, *you shall see My back but My face shall not be seen (Exodus 33:23).*

Moses had not known just how overwhelming it would be to see the glory of God. However, because God is a self-revealing God who wants to draw man to Himself, He showed as much of Himself to Moses as the prophet was able to bear. If God had shown more of Himself, Moses would have been utterly consumed by the brightness of His presence. Even though God did hide the fullness of His glory from Moses, when God passed by where Moses was He still had to shelter Moses in *the cleft* [crevice] *of a rock (Exodus 33:22).*

Living on the equator, my young friends were aware that they could not gaze at the brilliant light of the noonday sun without shielding their eyes. They also knew that moths were attracted to light on a dark night. When I asked what happens if the moths get too close to the source of light, their united reply was:

"They get killed." They were obviously aware of the dangers of an over-exposure to light.

I tried to think of another illustration that might help them to understand the answer to their question. All of my new young friends knew of the swaddling bands that swathed their baby brothers and sisters and secured them close to their mother's heart of love and tender care. I then told them of the swaddling band *(Job 38:9)* that God has wrapped around the earth.

(Scientists call it the ozone layer. This delicate blanket of allotropic oxygen filters out the harmful ultraviolet rays from the sun. Without the sun there would, of course, be no life on Planet Earth, but God's tender care has sheltered us from an overdose of the sun's energy and its cancer-causing effects.)

My little friends seemed particularly interested in God's swaddling band as I tried to explain in simple terms that it protects us all from terrible burns. I do not know whether they understood all I said, but their little hearts tenderly responded to the love and the glory of God and we had a precious time of prayer together. They evidently knew, in a personal way, that they too enjoyed the same protection that Moses had been given in his quest for God. And basic to our own understanding of what God is like, the Bible tells us that: "The Lord our God is **ONE Lord**" *(Deuteronomy 6:4 KJ)*. The oneness of His Person is a foundational truth.

But, to give us a fuller understanding of what He is like, God has also told us His names.

In the Bible, names are always considered important because their meaning is meant to reflect certain aspects of the bearer's character. Each name that is used to refer to God has a very special meaning and reveals a unique facet of His divine Person.

In the Old Testament there are three primary names that are used for God: Yahweh, Elohim and Adonai. Each has a special significance. Elohim is the first name to be used, and it is mentioned well over two thousand times. Though the name Yahweh is paramount, there is evidently also an importance and significance about His name Elohim that God does not want us to miss. What could this be?

In the English language, when we talk in the singular we speak of one and when we talk in the plural we refer to more than one. However, though we talk in the plural when we speak of more than 'one', the original Hebrew is more precise. It employs 'dual' when referring to 'two' and 'plural' when referring to more than two. The distinction between dual and plural (between 'two' and 'three or more') is very significant. Elohim is the first name in the Bible used for God. In Hebrew, Elohim—referring to the Creator-God—is neither singular nor dual but it is in the plural.

"In the beginning God [Elohim] created the heavens and the earth" (Genesis 1:1). So, we find, that in the very first verse of the Bible—which is God's revelation of Himself to man—there is the intimation of a three-in-one and one-in-three concept of who God is. This tri-unity has sometimes been called the Trinity.

After the first intimation of God's tri-unity we

come to the record of God's creation of man. "*And God said, Let Us make man in Our image*" *(Genesis 1:26).** Nobody can mistake that both 'Us' and 'Our' are plural pronouns in the English language. But, amazingly, in the very next sentence we read: "*Male and female He created them*" *(Genesis 1:27)*. Here, it is obvious that "He" can only refer to one person. So each of these references to God as 'one' and 'more than one' is to the God who has already introduced Himself as Elohim.

A God such as this is quite beyond the ability of worldly wisdom to comprehend. So, to help us in our understanding, God has graciously given "*the Spirit who is from God, that we might know the things freely given to us by God*" *(1 Corinthians 2:12)*. Commencing with these initial intimations of what God is like, the Bible gradually unfolds His mysterious tri-unity. To understand this three-in-one and one-in-three personality of who God is, will help you to appreciate more fully His astonishing love for you as you read chapter seven.

To help us comprehend something of the greatness of His love, God progressively reveals Himself throughout the rest of the Bible. There we are introduced to God the Father, to God the Son, and to God the Holy Spirit. Yet He reveals Himself to be only, and

---

* It is important to note that the creation of men and women can never be equated with the creation of the vegetable kingdom; nor even the highest form of evolutionary development in the animal kingdom. Not so, men and women were created in the "image of God" and are therefore a unique creation at the pinnacle of all God's marvelous creative acts. Later in this book, this uniqueness will assure you who you really are.

ever, one God. Our human minds can only grasp the fringes of such a concept. So, because it was impossible for man to reach up and discover the true and living God, He Himself took the initiative and introduced Himself to man.

The full revelation of God's glory and holiness was hidden from the eyes of Moses. However, in the person of God the Son, Elohim revealed as much of Himself to man as man could bear.

Accordingly in the New Testament we read:

> *God, who said, Light shall shine out of darkness, is the One who has shone in our hearts to give the light of the knowledge of the glory of God in the face of* [Jesus] *Christ (2 Corinthians 4:6).*

Just think of it: when John gazed into the face of Jesus Christ, he declared: *We beheld His glory, the glory as of the only begotten of the Father (John 1:14 KJ).*

Later John wrote of this, his personal encounter with God, and only because he had met Elohim in the person of Jesus, he lived to tell the story! Nevertheless, he made it quite clear that his encounter was in fact with the God of Eternity, the God of Creation, the God of Moses.

Astonishing as it was, this personal meeting between John and his Creator-God was audible, visible and tangible.

> *That which was from the beginning, which we have heard,* (his audible encounter) *which we have*

seen with our eyes (his visible encounter) ... *and our hands have handled* (his tangible encounter) *(1 John 1:1 KJ)*.

No, the record that we read in the epistle of John is not one of disrelated impersonal theology. It flows out of his own encounter with the living God.

"How does all this help me today?" you may ask. John is quick to answer that question. *These things write we unto you, that your joy may be full (1 John 1:4 KJ)*. And, likewise, this book you are now reading is in your hands because a friend longs that you, too, may have this fullness of joy as you meet the living God.

John explains:

That which we have seen and heard declare we unto you, that you also may have fellowship with us: and truly our fellowship is with the Father, and with His Son Jesus Christ. And these things write we unto you, that your joy may be full (1 John 1:3,4 KJ).

Yes, as light is attractive on a dark night, so the Light of God's Glory still draws men to Himself. Today in your desire to know what God is like, you too can pray with Moses: 'Show me Thy Glory.'

Pause to Consider

1. In your quest for God have you thoughtfully read the Bible?

2. Will you ask God to reveal Himself to you as you read the Bible?

   A suggested prayer: "O God, if You are the God who created this universe and who loves me, please reveal Yourself to me and show me if Jesus Christ is Your Son the promised Messiah!"

3. Do you recognize that if you are to truly worship God He must be:

   Greater than your ability to discover Him by human research; greater than your ability to fully comprehend Him in your human mind?

I think I understand somewhat of human nature, and I tell you all the heroes of antiquity were men, and I am a man; but not one is like him: Jesus Christ was more than a man.

NAPOLEON

Chapter 4

What really divides people?

he world of today has been described as a global village. However, because it is populated by hostile neighbors, this global village has become an increasingly dangerous place in which to live.

On the surface, it would appear that the problems that divide mankind cover a broad sweep of political, economic, domestic and even industrial issues. Though these problem areas do cause people to be increasingly and depressingly fragmented, there is an even greater, but less recognizable, reason for the alienation that exists in our world.

First, let us briefly consider the obvious causes of division among people, and then focus on the main cause.

Obvious Divisions

Politically: Politicians confront one another with fear and distrust. When faced with irreconcilable viewpoints, they hope that military might will guarantee their nation's future security.

Meanwhile, concerned citizens raise their voices in favor of peace and nuclear disarmament. Ironically, those of us who have seen some of these 'peace' demonstrations on television have witnessed that, in their conduct, participants sometimes display the very type of passion from which war is made.

Economically: Natural disasters such as drought, famine, starvation and earthquakes are an ever-increasing problem, particularly in the Third World. These disasters add to the pain caused by the great economic difference between rich and poor nations. In spite of the goodwill and sacrifice of many people who try to help, it is a sad observation that all too often the rich become richer and the poor poorer.

Domestically: It is no secret that today the breakdown of marriage and family life has reached epidemic proportions. With tears in his eyes, Letsoale said: "My house has been broken." I thought he meant that his four-walled African hut had been destroyed, but I soon learned that this expression of brokenness was Letsoale's delicate way of telling me that his wife had left him. Today, too many 'houses' are being 'broken', as selfish lifestyles destroy loving relationships. (However, as we shall see in a later chapter, the love of God is available to any couple who wish to cement their marriage in a permanent union.)

Industrially: In the workplace we become accustomed to hearing about dissatisfaction and tension. Early in

1985 the bitterest industrial dispute of the twentieth century was brought to a conclusion in Britain. Though the strike and the violent street confrontations ended, lingering resentments and bitterness continued to be an open sore in labor-management relations and within the industrial community itself. How different this situation is from the outcome of the labor-management tensions that were subdued in the coal mines of Wales after similar industrial unrest in 1904. John Parry told me the story from first-hand experience.

When I first met John, he was a 91-year-old retired coal miner, totally blind and suffering from a chronic lung problem called Miners' Disease. Whenever possible, my wife and I visited his humble miner's cottage in North Wales. With hearty laughter and vibrant joy, John delighted to recount to us what God had done in Wales when He moved in conviction and power during the Revival of 1904 and 1905. At that time both miners and their employers had met with the living God. As a direct result they had found real togetherness, mutual trust and respect. What a difference between 1905 and 1985.

John spoke with exuberant joy as he reflected on those days. He recalled that scores of 'public houses' went out of business because suddenly there was no demand for alcohol. He also recalled going down into the pits with his fellow miners as they unitedly sang the praises of God. He chuckled as he reflected: "People still come to see me and ask where the revival was." Thumping on his chest he would answer: "I tell 'em it's under here and it's right now!"

The Real Division

Deep as these divisions may be, there is something that divides mankind in a much more startling and permanent way. It is a danger that presently threatens to destroy the tranquillity of many lands. You see, people are ultimately polarized by their confused understanding about God!

In His revelation to mankind, God has never compromised the truth about His divine Being. Before Jesus Christ was born, God promised that He would send a great light to help people come to know Him as He really is. He said: *The people who walk in darkness will see a great light (Isaiah 9:2).* God also gave details as to how this light would be recognized: *for a child will be born . . . a Son will be given (Isaiah 9:6).*

Surely, there would be nothing particularly significant about that statement if God had only said that a child would be born. After all, children are always being born! Indeed, it would have been unimportant to record that a child was to be born if that fact had not been linked to the promise that a Son was to be given. And now what was once prophecy is history, for what God said would happen did happen. On earth a child was born; from Heaven a Son was given. Through the birth of a child who was the gift of a Son, God sent light to people who had been groping in darkness. Even to this very day that Light still dispels the darkness and doubt that would otherwise hide God from our eyes.

To distinguish the birth of God's unique child, and to set Him apart from all others, God promised that the birth of His Son would be authenticated by a miraculous 'sign': *Behold, a virgin will be with child and bear a son, and she will call His name Immanuel (Isaiah 7:14).*

How wonderful that His very name Immanuel means 'God with us.' And through what was conveyed by this name, we can begin to appreciate how the good news, as it is recorded in the Bible, is distinctive from the teachings of all other religions. Whereas false religions attempt to show how man is to reach up to God, the Bible is God's record of how He reached down to man.

As recorded in the Bible, when God established His beach-head on Planet Earth, a virgin was with child. And that day when the Creator of the universe condescended to become a part of time and space is now a matter of history: *An angel of the Lord appeared to him in a dream, saying, "Joseph, son of David, do not be afraid to take Mary as your wife; for that which has been conceived in her is of the Holy Spirit" (Matthew 1:20).* And later, after Jesus had been born and had matured to manhood, He further asserted His deity in the presence of hostile skeptics by saying: *I and My Father are one (John 10:30 KJ).*

Astronaut Jim Irwin of Apollo XV wrote: "God walking on earth is more important than man walking on the moon." Certainly no feat that man has accomplished in space can compare with the miracle of that moment when God stepped out of eternity into time.

After the prophecy that a child would be born and a Son would be given, there follows a more detailed prophetic 'résumé' of this unique Person: *"His name will be called Wonderful Counselor, Mighty God, Eternal Father, Prince of Peace. There will be no end to the increase of His government or of peace" (Isaiah 9:6,7).* Surely, such an awesome blend of power and purpose would be desirable if one were to become a successful world ruler. Even in today's world, we search for leaders who not only have the knowledge to do the right thing, but also the power to do it. Some leaders may have known what action should have been taken, but no leader in history has ever had the power and wisdom to produce a state of perpetual peace.

The Prince of Peace has both the knowledge and the power to bring permanent peace to this world. One day Jesus will return to rule on Planet Earth. When that day dawns, every armament factory will be closed; every unexploded nuclear bomb will be defused, and every border guard and soldier will be sent home for good!

Man has already demonstrated how hopelessly inadequate he is to govern the human race. Peace and justice for all must wait for the moment when the Prince of Peace Himself shall sway the scepter of a universal empire! Then men will *hammer their swords into plowshares, and their spears into pruning hooks. Nation will not lift up sword against nation, and never again will they learn war (Isaiah 2:4).* On that peaceful day: *the earth will be filled with the knowledge of the glory of the Lord, as the waters cover the sea (Habakkuk 2:14).* There can be no other conclusion to history that would satisfy the God of eternity.

But before that day of universal peace under the direction of the Lord Jesus, the deep and real division among people will be clearly seen. And the coming conflict will be centered around the person of Jesus Christ.

Therefore it is very important that you should be sure who Jesus is, why He came, and what He did for you when He was here.

The book of Genesis and the book of John begin in similar ways. In Genesis we read: I*n the beginning God created the heavens and the earth (Genesis 1:1).* In John we read: *In the beginning was the Word . . . and the Word was God. . . . All things were made by Him (John 1:1,3 KJ).* God, who is called Elohim in Genesis, is referred to as 'The Word' in the Gospel of John. Elohim is The Word, and He clothed Himself with flesh to walk among His own creation. The Word became flesh and dwelt among us. In its complete text this awesome statement reads:

> *In the beginning was the Word, and the Word was with God, and the Word was God. The same was in the beginning with God. All things were made by Him; and without Him was not anything made that was made . . . He was in the world, and the world was made by Him, and the world knew Him not. He came unto His own, and His own received Him not. But as many as received Him, to them gave He power to become the sons of God, even to them that*

believe on His name . . . And the Word was made
flesh, and dwelt among us (and we beheld His glory,
the glory as of the only begotten of the Father), full
of grace and truth . . . (John 1:1-3, 10-12,14 KJ).

Like Moses many centuries earlier and like people
of all times, the Disciple Philip also desired to know
what God was like.

Philip made a special request of Jesus when he
said: *Lord, show us the Father (John 14:8).* Surpris-
ingly enough, Jesus answered: *He who has seen Me*
has seen the Father (John 14:9). Such an astonishing reply would make Jesus seem like an idiot or a
deceiver, unless He were God Himself. No one would
seriously accuse Him of either of the first two. If He
were not God, He would be the biggest impostor that
the world has ever known. So we must accept that
when we look on Jesus we see God.

It is at this point—the declaration of who Jesus
is—that people begin to part company. In one sense, it
is not surprising that when Jesus said: *I and the Father*
are one (John 10:30), some found in Him the answer
to their quest for God. However, others who could not
conceive of the possibility of God humbling Himself
in such a way reacted with hostility. Jesus attracted
some, but He alienated others; though there were those
who followed Him, there were others who plotted His
death.

Even in His lifetime Jesus divided people. He
clearly stated:

He who is not with Me is against Me (Matthew 12:30).

However, an initial reaction need not be a permanent response.

Let us consider one man who turned from being a foe of Jesus to being His follower. In his early days Saul, a Jewish rabbi, hated the followers of Jesus so much that he persecuted them and even consented to their death. But, after being converted, he spent his remaining years honoring Jesus as his Lord and Master. Eventually, he joyfully suffered great hardship because of his loyalty to Christ. What made the difference?

When Saul was journeying to Damascus, he saw a "great light." That light was so brilliant that he was temporarily blinded. Saul intuitively knew, however, that he was in the presence of God.

Using the Greek word for Yahweh, he asked: *Who art Thou, Lord?* God replied: *I am Jesus whom you are persecuting (Acts 9:5).* That day Saul learned that Yahweh and Jesus are one.

This revelation changed Saul from being an enemy of Jesus into Paul the Apostle. From that day on, he completely committed his life to the Lord Jesus Christ. Though he suffered much for his faith, he spent the rest of his life spreading the Good News that God had visited Planet Earth. The reality of Jesus Christ in Paul's life transformed him into the greatest missionary of all times. His letters are full of his convictions that all things were created by, and for, the Lord Jesus

Christ *(Colossians 1:16)*.

As we have seen, the Bible declares that Jesus of Nazareth is God **the** Son, not just **a** son of God as Mormons, Jehovah's Witnesses and many others believe. Nor was He just **a** prophet of God as Islam teaches. In an effort to include the false teachings of such groups many choose to ignore the revelation that God has given of Himself. This is known as 'syncretism,' which is defined in *Webster's Dictionary* as the "attempt to combine differing beliefs."

Hindus, for example, acknowledge 'Jesus' by simply adding Him to their shelf alongside their many other 'gods'. We do well to remember that when Elijah's God, the true and living God, confronted the pagan idols of Baal, He knocked them flat on their faces before Him. In like manner every man-made and man-conceived god must fall before the Lord Jesus Christ, for He is God the Son, eternally one with the Father and with the Holy Spirit.

Once we understand that Jesus Christ is God, we should have no difficulty believing in His virgin birth, His many miracles, His death and resurrection, His ascension into Heaven, and His soon return to earth in power and glory. Because Jesus Christ is 'Very God,' the creator of the universe with all its laws and life-support systems, He transcends every law that He Himself created for His own purposes of love and redemption.

Around the person of Jesus of Nazareth, the world is divided. The separated groups alienated from one another do not consist of the 'have's' and the 'have not's,' nor the politically strong and the politically weak, nor even nations with different ideologies. The real division that exists, which was caused when God visited this earth, is far more fundamental than all of the other issues that divide humanity.

This definitive statement is not an over dramatization of the facts, for the Lord Jesus Himself said:

> *If God were your Father, you would love Me; for I proceeded forth and have come from God, for I have not even come on My own initiative, but He sent Me. Why do you not understand what I am saying? It is because you cannot hear My word. You are of your father the devil, and you want to do the desires of your father. He was a murderer from the beginning, and does not stand in the truth, because there is no truth in him. Whenever he speaks a lie, he speaks from his own nature; for he is a liar, and the father of lies (John 8:42-44).*

Does it come as a surprise to learn that just as there is a family of believers whose Father is God, so, too, there is a family of unbelievers whose father is the Devil? Not everyone is a child of God. To be in the family of God or in the family of Satan, these are the eternal alternatives for you and for me.

Regardless of how sincere your belief about God may be, you can still be 'sincerely' wrong. It is a lie to say that it does not matter what a person believes, provided he is sincere. In like manner, you could eat poison while sincerely believing that it was medicine, but you would still die!

Truly, the human race is divided into two families. Every person belongs to either one or other of these two families: the Family of God or the family of the Devil. It is very important that you know to whose family you belong. And the first step in becoming a member of God's family is an understanding of who God is and what He has done in giving us His Son, Jesus.

The name 'Jesus' means 'Yahweh is salvation.' So the angel said to Joseph: . . . *you shall call His name JESUS, for it is He who will save His people from their sins (Matthew 1:21).*

Pause to Consider

1. As long as you are sincere, does it really matter what you believe about God?

2. What is the ultimate cause of division among people? Is it political, economic, domestic or industrial? Or is it spiritual and eternal?

3. To which one of the two families that the Lord Jesus described do you want to belong?

In a deep sense [awareness] of moral evil, more perhaps than anything else, abides a saving knowledge of God.

DR. ARNOLD (HEADMASTER RUGBY PUBLIC SCHOOL)

What is the real problem?

At the beginning of the twentieth century many people were very optimistic about the future of this world. They believed that it was about to enter a golden age of peace and prosperity. Many thought that the blessings of this new era would be seen in every country, even the countries where despair, disease and extreme poverty had inflicted indescribable suffering. But in 1914 the sirens of war sounded throughout Europe.

And today, as the twenty-first century unfolds, in spite of the incredible scientific breakthroughs that we have witnessed, people no longer seem to talk about a bright tomorrow. Instead, millions worry about the overkill capabilities of the world's arsenal of nuclear weapons. The complexity of both international terrorism and national problems cause many thoughtful observers to conclude that we live in the most critical and potentially dangerous years of human history. We have already considered the polarization of people in today's world. The very fiber of a civilized society is under attack. What went wrong?

In an effort to answer this question, notable world leaders meet and talk. As they air the issues and listen to each other's theories and proposals, the world moves on from one crisis to another. Regardless of the amount of energy and money invested, nobody seems able to change the direction that the world is heading. Distinguished statesmen and politicians, brilliant scientists and scholars, shrewd businessmen and world bankers, revered doctors and sociologists all contribute their particular expertise. Still, no answer is found.

And from these learned men, there is seldom, if ever, a reference made to what God declares to be the real problem of man—the basic problem that must be identified before a solution can be found. Only God can make us aware of our real problem. And it is at this point that we often recognize the difference between those who really search for God and those who only have a religious curiosity.

God said: *Let Us make man in Our own image (Genesis 1:26).* You may ask: "In what way was man created in God's image?" Certainly not in physical likeness, for the Lord Jesus said: *God is Spirit (John 4:24).* God does not have arms and legs and eyes as we do. And this God *dwells in unapproachable light; whom no man has seen or can see (1 Timothy 6:16).* An invisible man has never existed. Therefore there must be something more valuable about people than the bodies they live in! It is this real person that lives on when the body gives up—the 'person' that was created after God's likeness.

The Bible reveals that God has a mind, emotions and a will. And it is in these three areas that man was created in God's image. Because He is God, however, His intellect, emotions and volition are infinite; in other words, without any limit. Such is His nature. By contrast, however, man is finite. Even the brilliant Einstein had a finite mind. No man can know everything, no man can love without limit, and certainly the will of man is not sovereign in the universe. He is not the master of his fate, nor is he the captain of his destiny.

Man's personality, on the other hand, has a spiritual capacity in order that he may know and have fellowship with God. That is why the Bible makes it clear that man is *spirit and soul and body (1 Thessalonians 5:23)*.

Through his spirit, man has the God-given potential to be intimately related to his Creator. Through his body, man's personality (or soul i.e., or his capacity to think, choose and love) is related to the material world.

As long as we note the Biblical record of priorities which places the spirit first, the soul second and the body third, all is well!

But something went wrong. As a result, for many people, the order is reversed: the body becomes priority number one; the soul priority number two; and the spirit number three. Unfortunately in today's world, many people's physical, material and sensual interests dominate their thinking, their decisions and their affections, while their spiritual capacity lies dormant and dead. So, instead of God being permitted to restore spiritual life and control the very person He created, He is subordinated, or even dismissed, to the extent that there can be no communication between these misguided people and their Creator.

The person to whom God is distant and unreal is actually dead spiritually. On the other hand, the person who enjoys fellowship with God is truly and completely alive.

> *But God, being rich in mercy, because of His great love with which He loved us, **even when we were dead** in our transgressions, made us alive together with Christ (Ephesians 2:4,5).*

The problems of this world all began in the will of man. God did not create people to be like puppets, which are unable to move without the will of another. By pulling the strings, the puppeteer controls every movement the puppet makes. God, on the other hand, has given us a free will to behave as we choose. But with the gift of that will, we also become morally responsible for the decisions we make. (That is hardly what you will hear from many psychiatrists who ignore Bible truth.)

A tragedy of the first order happened in the human race after man was created. Among the trees in the Garden of Eden there were two special ones. One was called *The Tree of Life*; the other, *The Tree of the Knowledge of Good and Evil. (Genesis 2:9).* Adam and Eve were told by God that they could eat from all the trees except from the The Tree of the Knowledge of Good and Evil. By giving them this choice, a choice between obedience and disobedience, God made it very clear that He had created man—man and woman—with a free will. It was up to them whether they wanted to obey God or not. This was their own, personal decision.

Sadly, Adam and Eve rebelled against the very best that God had made available to mankind. God knew ahead of time that their decision to be disobedient would bring to Himself indescribable suffering, and that it would bring pain to all mankind. But, in His love for His creation and knowing the glory that would later be available to those who would make the right choice, God has given to every person the freedom to choose.

Satan, the liar, used his persuasive influence to tempt Adam and Eve to make the wrong choice. He glamorized the forbidden fruit by suggesting that if they were to eat it they would be like God. (Satan still suggests that man can be his own god. But just as God is God and can never be less than God, so man is man and can never be more than man). However, Satan seduced Adam and Eve into exerting their will against the will of God. As a result, each new generation of people is cut off from a vital, personal and intimate fellowship with the Creator, for all are the descendants of Adam. And: *just as through one man sin entered into the world, and death through sin, and so death spread to all men, because all sinned (Romans 5:12).*

Every cemetery, every hospital, every army and every prison that the world has ever known is the result of man's wrong choice at the beginning of creation. This deadly evil in the human race, which we call sin, is an inborn disease affecting all mankind. Not only has sin severed man's true fellowship with God, but it has also separated him from his fellow man.

But, you and I are not only sinners by birth; we are also sinners by deed.

As far as our birth is concerned, the Psalmist spoke for us all when he said: *Behold, I was shapen in iniquity; and in sin did my mother conceive me (Psalm 51:5 KJ)*. But that sin-inherited condition does not provide an excuse for the acts of sin that we all have committed. The Bible also states that we are—*the children of **disobedience** . . . fulfilling the desires of the flesh and of the mind; and were by nature the children of wrath, even as others (Ephesians 2:2,3 KJ)*.

Yes, we are guilty before God because of our own disobedience. No one else can be blamed—not a wife nor a friend nor a parent. Even the background we come from and the environment in which we live cannot be faulted. You are responsible for your own sin, even as I am for mine.

The real reason that we see so much hostility and division between people is that sin is the common denominator of us all. Sin ties an atheist to a believer and an Arab to a Jew. Sin ties people in the Third World to people in the industrial world. Sin ties a communist to a capitalist, a policeman to a criminal, and a feminist to a male chauvinist. Whether people are prostitutes or preachers, whether they live in the height of luxury or the depth of poverty, whether they are educated or illiterate *all have sinned, and fall short of the glory of God (Romans 3:23).* And sin is the basic cause of all the tensions that exist among men.

But Jesus is the sinner's hope! He said: *I am not come to call the righteous, but sinners to repentance (Matthew 9:13 KJ).* Whether by a short or great distance, you and I have missed the mark of God's holiness. The word 'sin' simply means 'to miss the mark.' By ourselves we can do nothing to correct that. It is a vain hope to think that we can find peace with God either by being good or doing good. It is: *not as a result of works, that no one should boast (Ephesians 2:9).* That is why when talking of salvation, Jesus said: *I will have mercy, and not sacrifice (Matthew 9:13 KJ).*

A true understanding of the mercy of God brings overwhelming relief to people gripped by the seriousness of their personal sin.

Because God is *rich in mercy (Ephesians 2:4),* all that He asks is that you receive salvation as His free gift. *For by grace are ye saved through faith; and that not of yourselves: **it is the gift of God** (Ephesians 2:8 KJ).* Jesus himself paid the supreme sacrifice to open the door for a sinner to enter God's holy presence.

The God of mercy has now made abundant life freely available through the Lord Jesus Christ. But, because He has given you a will, God will not compel you to partake of that life. How you respond to God's offer of His free gift is a matter of great urgency. God says: *now is the acceptable time, behold, now is the day of salvation (2 Corinthians 6:2).* Now—not sometime in the future after you have tried to straighten out your life by yourself. Remember that Jesus said: *I did not come to call the righteous, but sinners (Matthew 9:13).*

To be honest about your real problem, the problem of sin, is the first step towards its solution. The arms of Jesus are open to receive you today, wherever you are and in whatever condition or state you are in. All He wants to hear from you is: *God, be merciful to me, the sinner (Luke 18:13).*

A Letter from "C Max Prison"

The following unedited quotes were received from a prisoner in the highest security prison in South Africa.

"The Book Your Quest for God ... *help me to understand the Word of God. I mean this book help us to find the true way of life. I do believe you understand me. My friend gave me this book ... I believe God is creator and he creator all the universe. I believe God will help me as now I'm in prison..."*

– Report submitted by Trans World Radio

Pause to Consider

1. Do you perceive that today there is something tragically wrong with society?

2. When you are ill, is it vital that your doctor correctly diagnoses your sickness before giving you medicine?

3. How does the Bible: Diagnose your problem? Prescribe the remedy for your problem?

Now there was a certain man named Simon, who formerly was practicing magic in the city, and astonishing the people of Samaria, claiming to be someone great; and they all, from the smallest to the greatest, were giving attention to him, saying, 'This man is what is called the Great Power of God.'

DR. LUKE

Chapter 6

Why are people so misguided?

s a boy, I lived in a part of the British Isles over which enemy bombers continually flew. It was wartime, and these bombers were en route to their target areas in the industrial Midlands and Northern England. My friends and I learned to distinguish the drone of an enemy bomber from the roar of our own fighter planes. When we saw the searchlights illuminate an enemy plane in the skies, we became very excited. We knew the 'Ack-Ack' guns on the ground or a 'dog fight' in the air would sometimes result in a bomber being shot down.

With the shooting down of an enemy plane, there was always the possibility that some of the crew members would parachute to safety. To make it difficult for the survivors to find their way and thereby escape and perhaps return with another load of bombs, the authorities dismantled the signposts at the road intersections. Thus there were virtually no signposts on the roads.

However, we boys knew that outside of town, in Wootten Woods, there still remained a small signpost at a very insignificant intersection. When we turned that signpost around and pointed it in the wrong direction, we really thought we were helping the war effort. We, like the local authorities, wanted to confuse any unwelcome guests on our shores.

Of course, if such a person held a reliable map in his hands, the fact that there were no signposts would have presented no problem. Even our boyish idea of turning the signpost around would not have confused the enemy unless he had chosen to ignore the information on his map.

God tells us the kinds of people who, in their quest for God, will be misguided by a false signpost.

To begin with, any person who chooses to ignore the fact that the existence of this marvelous universe points to the Creator God will really become confused!

> *Professing to be wise, they became fools . . . And just as they did not see fit to acknowledge God any longer, God gave them over to a depraved mind . . . (Romans 1:22,28).*

And that depraved mind will worship the works of creation, instead of the Creator Himself. A clear thinking man, on the other hand, will worship his Creator. Thus, if you refuse to believe that God created the universe, God will give you over to a corrupt mind and let you believe some wild idea about how the universe came into being. A depraved mind is a deluded mind!

God also warns that people who refuse to accept the Word of God as truth will readily follow a deceptive path, one which will lead to destruction. Indeed, any person who chooses not to positively and actively love the truth of God's Word puts himself in a very dangerous position.

Because they did not receive the love of the truth so as to be saved . . . God will send upon them a deluding influence so that they might believe what is false . . . (2 Thessalonians 2:10,11).

Once a person has ignored or rejected the truth, he will readily embrace that which is false.

I well remember once when I tried to find my way home through a dense London fog. Just to find my way to the edge of the road, I needed all the help I could get. Even the light of my flashlight could not be seen when I held it out at arm's length. God tells us that a strong delusion, which is really like a mental fog, will accompany the end of this present order of things on Planet Earth, for the people will have rejected the truth of God's Word. The disciples of Jesus asked Him, *what will be the sign of Your coming, and of the end of the age?* Among other things He answered:

For false Christs and false prophets will arise and will show great signs and wonders, so as to mislead, if possible, even the elect (Matthew 24:24).

Even now you may be saying to yourself: "Well, I am not deceived." You may even take pride in the fact that you can easily recognize a false Christ or a false prophet. But stop for a moment and think about your conclusion. If, because you have not loved the truth, God has allowed Satan to deceive your mind, you would certainly not be aware of it. If you actually knew that some false prophet had deceived you, you would not really be deceived at all. All delusion must be in the mind, and anyone who is intellectually proud will find it hard to accept that his mind has been tricked into believing a lie.

There are really two types of people who will resist truth when they read the Bible, thereby opening themselves up to the deceptions taught by the world. One is the person who is intellectually proud and seemingly self-sufficient. The other is the person who is morally disobedient. But to every person who really desires to do the will of God, the Lord Jesus has a special promise: *"If any man desires to do His will, he will know ... whether the teaching is from God or whether I am speaking from Myself..." (John 7:17 Amp).*

If you really desire to do the will of God, you may be assured that through the Bible God will teach you what to believe and what not to believe, and how to behave and how not to behave.

However, we still must be careful to reject the words of those self-appointed religious teachers who do not teach the true Word of God, but will instead try to get you to believe and do the wrong things.

In this generation, some of Satan's agents who point people in the wrong direction are members of pseudo-Christian cults. Any person who has chosen to reject the truth about God the Father, God the Son and God the Holy Spirit—Three in One and One in Three—is a false prophet. Though such people may quote a few isolated verses from the Bible, they totally divorce the text from the context and so promote a non-Biblical religion. You can always detect a false teacher by asking him: "Who is Jesus Christ?" That is part of the reason why it is so important that you know who He is.

When you indeed know Jesus to be God the Son, even the secret societies that have such a great camaraderie of helping one another will be seen as yet another spiritual delusion.* While God may be mentioned in

---

* Freemasonry is the largest international secret society in the world, presently boasting a membership of about ten million men around the world. Though its principles of 'Brotherly love, relief, and truth' seem attractive to many, Masonry is not as harmless as it may appear to the uninitiated. To become a Mason, each candidate must confess that he is in darkness reaching for the light. A follower of Jesus already believes he has found the light. Jesus said: I am the light of the world; he who follows Me shall not walk in the darkness, but shall have the *light of life* (John 8:12). The initiation ceremony into the Masonic secret society is very dramatic and full of symbolism. At that time, the Masonic candidate is guided away from Biblical concept of God, when he is introduced to the name of 'Gauto.' The candidate is told that Gauto is "the lost name for God," and that Gauto is "the grand architect of the universe." In theory, any believer in God whether Buddhist, Hindu, Muslim, Jewish or Christian can become a Freemason. So Gauto (a man-made concept of God) deflects the thoughts of the candidate from Jesus, who the Bible declares is *the true Light* (John 1:9). Later, when the Mason becomes a Master Mason, he is taught a further name for God—'Jahbulon.' This name is really a combination of Jewish and Middle Eastern names for God. It is derived from JAH for YAHWEH, BUL (a form of Baal) and ON, which refers to the Egyptian Sun-god. This is a classic example of syncretism, with its vain attempts to combine differing beliefs. Jesus Himself stated: *If therefore the light that is in you is darkness, how great is the darkness*! (Matthew 6:23).

such societies, these groups ignore the teachings of Jesus Christ, who said:

> *No one comes to the Father, but through Me (John 14:6).* The Bible records scathing words concerning those who have a misguided belief about God. *Thou believest that there is one God; thou doest well: the devils also believe, and tremble (James 2:19 KJ).*

Today we are also seeing an alarming growth of activity from the major religions that deny the God of the Bible. Various sects of the Hindu religion are attracting the interest and following of many new people. In countries once known for their Biblical heritage, the basic Hindu philosophy is presented in the form of Transcendental Meditation or such forms of Eastern Mysticism as yoga and asceticism. The various cults that have sprung from Hinduism fool-ishly worship many gods in creation, rather than the God of Creation. And, sad to say, many deluded minds are more fascinated by a self-exalted 'Guru' than they are with the God of Creation who humbled Himself to visit Planet Earth.

The Muslim world is also displaying tremendous zeal in spreading its faith. Their oil dollars and their growing political clout enable them to expand their borders on a scale thought impossible but a few years ago. From one of their most 'holy' shrines, called the Dome of the Rock and located on the Temple Mount in Jerusalem, they boldly deny the very heart of God's good news. The Arabic caption surrounding the Dome of the Rock states: "God is not begotten, neither can He Beget." The Bible, however, states:

*For God so loved the world, that He gave His **only begotten Son,** that whoever believes in Him should not perish, but have eternal life (John 3:16).*

And spiritual delusion is not confined to the religious world. The secular world has embraced a humanistic philosophy which holds that man is the center of the universe and that society's supreme goal is the development of man. Humanism is proclaimed in universities, newspapers, multi-national corporate seminars, popular magazines, and on radio and television. 'Pamper yourself' is the selfish theme popularized by the advertising world.

Humanism, which is nothing more than the worshiping of man, is really not as new a philosophy as some may think. Back in Paul's day, God said: *They exchanged the truth of God for a lie, and worshipped and served the creature rather than the Creator . . . (Romans 1:25).* The Lord asks what must surely be a very humbling question to humanists: *Where were you when I laid the foundation of the earth! Tell me if you have understanding (Job 38:4).* It is the old story. When Satan came to Eve, he posed an impossibility as a possibility by saying: *you will be like God (Genesis 3:5).* In our day Satan continues his nasty work through the deceptive teachings of secular humanism.

Maybe you are a modern youth who is not 'turned on' either by the political or the religious scene. To you, politicians are suspect and religion is irrelevant.

You prefer to join with your peers and look elsewhere for personal fulfillment. You may think that the life-style described by the lyrics of 'punk rock,' 'new wave music,' 'heavy metal,' or whatever else is on the scene will give you an escape from the lonely world in which you find yourself.

You are, of course, aware of the words that you listen and dance to. Though you might not want to describe them in this way, surely you will agree that for the most part they are a combination of Satanism, sadism and sex. Not infrequently the horrors of Hell are presented in the music as an attractive alternative to a supposedly meaningless existence. In an atmosphere that sometimes reaches frenzied violence, the banner under which these young people unite encourages them to destroy themselves and one another.

Let me tell you of a place in the city of Los Angeles. It is a mortuary called 'The Refrigerator.' There, 600 bodies, many of them young people, are stored for three months in the hope that someone will be able to identify them. 'Anonymous' tags are tied to their toes. The vast majority of these unfortunates are eventually buried as unidentified 'John Does' in paupers' graves. Most of them have come from the drug scene, having acted upon the same message that is presently being proclaimed from discos and listened to on CD players in millions of homes. They had followed the wrong signpost. Now, at the end of the road, it is too late to change. If only they had heard and heeded the words of the Lord Jesus, Who said: *I came that they might have **life**, and might have it abundantly (John 10:10).*

And now added to all this confusion is the phenomenal growth of interest in the 'black arts'. Reliable sources indicate that active interest in the occult is as prevalent today as it was in what is known as the Dark Ages. And this occurs in spite of today's so-called 'scientific enlightenment'.

In the most unlikely places there are growing numbers of Satan worshippers. Professionals from the City of London assemble in Kensington to celebrate the 'Black Mass.' Witches' covens have proliferated in Europe as well as in such remote places as beautiful Vancouver Island. The dark practices of ancestral worship from Africa are being duplicated in spiritistic seances throughout the world. Various parlor games such as 'Dungeons and Dragons' and the 'Ouija Board' cater to people's growing fascination with evil and the supernatural. Such proliferating phenomena are the result of a superficial spiritual curiosity. In their misguided quest for God, many people, not only turn **from** the light of God, but they also turn **to** the darkness of the occult for some sort of false, empty spiritual fulfillment. And all this takes place in what we still call the civilized world.

We do well to remember what God says about the last days. He warns us about *false prophets* and the spurious *signs and wonders* that would accompany the great delusion of the end times. In fact, God tells us that there is going to appear a master of deception, whose sinister deeds will be *in accordance with the work of Satan and displayed in all kinds of counterfeit miracles, signs and wonders, and in every sort of evil that deceives those who are perishing (2 Thessalonians 2:9,10 NIV).*

Because of this accelerating interest in false teachings and evil practices, it is not hard to understand why a growing number of nations and communities are blanketed with the oppressive forces of skepticism, empty resignation and hopelessness. Satan's signposts are too many to mention, but you can be sure that none of them point to the Lord Jesus Christ as the only deliverer of men.

God's message, contrary to the world's dismal portrayal of life, is certainly not one of gloom, confusion and death. His is a message of hope, assurance and vibrant life as it is found in Christ. As you read the Bible in your quest for God, the Holy Spirit will always point you to the Lord Jesus Christ, who said: *I am the way, and the truth, and the Life.* And there can be no other, for Jesus continues: *No one comes to the Father, but through Me (John 14:6).*

God has warned you about the deceptive signposts so that you will not be misguided. He has also informed you about the growing delusion that could cloud your thinking. Now He gives you this promise:

'For I know the plans that I have for you . . . plans for welfare and not for calamity to give you a future and a hope. Then you will call upon Me and come and pray to Me, and I will listen to you. And you will seek Me and find Me, when you search for Me with all your heart. And I will be found by you, 'declares the Lord' (Jeremiah 29:11-14).

Pause to Consider

1. What kind of a mind will worship creation rather than the Creator? *(Read Romans 1:22-28)*

2. In your quest for God, what is the key that will unlock any intellectual problem you have? *(Read John 7:17)*

   Is it your mind?

   Is it your desire and will?

3. Has God given you a clear 'signpost' to guide you to Himself? *(Read John 8:12)*

Many years ago a lad in a Sunday School class in England asked his Sunday School teacher: "Does God love naughty boys?" and the teacher said, "No, Certainly Not." Oh, the unintentional blasphemy of telling a boy that! If God did not love naughty boys, He would never have loved me! Shakespeare says: 'Love is not love that alters when it alteration finds'.

G. CAMPBELL MORGAN

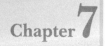

Chapter 7

Does God truly love me?

*H*ave you ever questioned the love of some-body who is very important to you? Or have you ever tried to prove that you love somebody when they did not believe it? In either case, you will know that there are times when true love can better be expressed by deeds than by words.

Since deeds are so much more powerful than words, God demonstrated His love for you by what He did when Jesus died upon the Cross. When you understand the significance of this, you will need no other explanation to help you understand that God really does love you.

Just after I was converted to Christ, I read the true story of a young bugle boy and a soldier. They both served in the army during the Boer War. The bugle boy, Willie Holt, was twelve years old when he was assigned to a tent with seven godless soldiers. One of these men was called Bill. However, unlike Bill, Willie was a devoted believer in the Lord Jesus Christ. Each night, he knelt by his bed to silently pray and read his Bible. As he did so, the other soldiers mocked and cursed.

One day the Colonel-in-Charge called the Company on parade. A thief had been traced to the tent where Willie and Bill had been assigned. In a desperate attempt to trace the criminal, the Colonel issued his ultimatum to the whole Company: "My previous warnings have been to no avail," he said. "Last night the thief was at it again. Today, I will give the culprit one last opportunity to identify himself and take his punishment like a man. If he does not respond, every man in the Company will be punished with ten lashes of the whip upon his bare back. But if one of you comes forward to take the punishment, the rest will be spared."

After a tense silence, Willie stood to attention, stepped forward and said: "Sir, you have just stated that, 'if one man comes forward to take the punishment the rest will be spared.' Sir, I will be that man." With anger, the Colonel cried out against the unknown coward: "How can you let an innocent lad take your punishment?" No one moved. "Then," said the Colonel, "you will all watch the wretched sight of an innocent boy taking punishment for the guilty man."

True to his word, the Colonel ordered Willie's back to be bared, and then the cruel lashes of the whip commenced. As Willie fainted beneath the bitter blows, suddenly Bill, unable to bear the spec-tacle any longer, rushed from the ranks and shouted: "Stop! I am the thief. I will take my own punishment." Coming round from his swoon, Willie tenderly lifted his eyes to Bill and whispered: "It's all right Bill, the Colonel can't go back on his word now. I will take all of your punishment." And he did!

Young Willie never did recover from the effects of his lashing. But before Willie went to Heaven, Bill, now a broken man, wept at his bed-side and asked: "Why Willie? Why did you do it for me? I'm not worth it." Willie's answer was simple and telling: "Bill," he said, "I have often tried to tell you how much God loves you but you always laughed; I thought that if I took your punishment, it might help you to understand how much Jesus loved you when He went to the Cross to take your place and to die for your sin." Before Willie went to Heaven, Bill accepted the salvation so freely offered by a loving Christ.

In Christ, Heaven launched its triumphant rescue operation for lost humanity. And it was Love—the love of God for each of us—that prompted Christ's incredible act of sacrifice and suffering.

The Perfect Man

Three crosses were erected on the hill of Golgotha. On two of them, thieves were crucified. Between these criminals the Lord Jesus was nailed, and there He died.

During his last hours of excruciating suffering, one of the thieves ventured to express his opinion about the quasi-judicial system under which all three had been condemned to die. Amazing as it may seem, his primary concern was not for his own pain-racked and tortured body. Instead, his thoughts turned to how the Roman judiciary was out of line in condemning Jesus to the same death as the two thieves. It was this glaring injustice that seemed to trouble him. Lucidly and humbly, the dying thief made three very astute observations as he approached his final moment.

First: *We are receiving what we deserve for our deeds.* In that brief and humble statement, the dying thief confessed his personal responsibility for his crime, and therefore acknowledged his own personal guilt.

Second: *And we indeed die justly. . .* In our day when petty-pilfering and even violent acts of robbery are commonplace, it may be difficult to understand how seriously such crimes were viewed in the first century. But in three brief words, the dying thief expressed his conviction that, in his day, his sentence of death was both legal and just. *We . . . die justly.*

Third: *This man has done nothing wrong.* Although it is remarkable to read how the thief acknowledged his own personal guilt and how he had accepted the justice of the legal system, it is quite astonishing to read of his concern for Jesus, who hung on the cross beside him. *This man*—this Jesus, the dying thief observed, was guiltless and therefore had been unjustly condemned to die.

Being convicted of his own sin, as he hung upon the cross the thief had no other hope but to turn to Jesus. So he then earnestly pleaded: *Jesus remember me when You come in Your Kingdom.* Responding, as He always does, to such an honest confession of guilt and need, the Lord Jesus immediately promised: *Today you shall be with Me in Paradise (Luke 23:39-43)*.

That day, the dying thief, like all repentant sinners who turn to the Lord, was assured of eternal life. He had turned to the right person—the Lord Jesus Christ—and had asked for His mercy at the right place—the Cross where Jesus died.

Yes, on that awesome day, in the eyes of one of the dying thieves, the Lord Jesus was indeed **guiltless**. However, at a later time two disciples were even more specific in their observations. They testified that Jesus was **sinless**. Each of these disciples, together with the Apostle Paul, recorded his own personalized testimonial to Jesus' sinlessness.

PETER, a close friend of the Lord Jesus, was known as a man of impetuous action. Therefore, when he testified to the sinlessness of Jesus, in accord with his personality, he used an action word: *He* (the Lord Jesus) *did no sin (1 Peter 2:22 KJ)*.

JOHN also had a very special friendship with the Lord Jesus. Consequently he frequently had the opportunity to observe his Lord when he was away from the critical scrutiny of the crowds. From this vantaged perspective John clearly testified that: *in Him* (the Lord Jesus) *is no sin (1 John 3:5 KJ)*.

PAUL, on the other hand, was known as a scholar of some exceptional renown. Therefore, when Paul, a man of learning and knowledge, spoke of the Lord

Jesus it is not surprising that he declared: He *knew no sin (2 Corinthians 5:21).* Such a triad of authentic testimony concerning Christ's sinless life is most impressive.

But some may want to dismiss these astute observations, saying, "Aha, neither the dying thief nor the apostles Peter, John or Paul, could be described as objective witnesses. The dying thief was a desperate man and the apostles were prejudiced by their devotion to the Lord Jesus." Well then, how about Pontius Pilate, the Roman Governor of Judea? Certainly, he was no friend of Christ. Nevertheless, when answering the accusers of Jesus who had trumped up a false charge against Him with the intent of securing His death, Pilate declared:

> *I, having examined Him before you, have found no fault in this man touching those things whereof you accuse Him (Luke 23:14 KJ).*

But what are all these human testimonials when we compare them with the declaration of God the Father from His Throne in Heaven? When a person is about to speak at a public gathering, it is considered right and proper that such a one should be politely introduced. Likewise, when Jesus was about to commence His own public ministry, God the Father reserved for Himself the privilege of introducing His beloved Son. With a clarion voice from Heaven, the Father announced: *This is My beloved Son, in whom I am well-pleased (Matthew 3:17).*

The Father knew that while Jesus had been in this

world in human form He had lived as God had created man to live. Every other person has fallen *short of the glory of God (Romans 3:23).* But not Jesus! He was perfect in every way. Therefore, when Jesus was about to begin His public ministry, His Father introduced Him, and it was His *Holy Father (John 17:11)* who expressed good pleasure at the way His beloved Son had lived.

As we have already explained, the Lord Jesus was never ever less than God. It is therefore awesome to realize that God had humbled Himself and, having condescended to be born through the womb of a virgin mother, had taken upon Himself the form of man. However, if Jesus as man had not been totally submissive to His Heavenly Father, He could never have brought undiluted pleasure to His Father. Yet, throughout His earthly pilgrimage Jesus was always obedient to, and dependent upon, His Father. Thus His humanity became the earthly expression of His Heavenly Father's holiness, love and purpose in a world of suffering, selfishness and sin.

Yes, as man, Jesus walked upon the very planet that He, as God, had created. Although the Lord Jesus was never less than God, for 33 years He showed man how God had intended man to live. Nothing in the humanity of Jesus ever violated what God had made man to be. During those years, He was always totally available to His Father in Heaven. Therefore, the Father was *well pleased* when He gazed upon His own beloved Son, who lived as the **perfect** man among men.

Guiltless! Sinless! Perfect! To the dying thief and Pontius Pilate, Jesus was guiltless. To Peter, John and Paul, Jesus was sinless. To the Holy Father in Heaven, Jesus was perfect. Guiltless! Sinless! Perfect!—And yet He died: died for us because of His great love for each of us!

Love Without Limit

Now, in your imagination, try to join those spectators who viewed the terrible events of that first 'Good Friday.' Around the Cross the crowd gaped. And as they watched the horrific spectacle, they were confronted with a shocking scene of gory contrast.

On either side of Jesus there hung a criminal. Both of these men were guilty before their fellow-men, and both were guilty before their Creator God. For them both the penalty of death was required by the law of the land.

Between these two men, Jesus hung upon His own Cross. In vivid contrast to the thieves, Jesus was not only guiltless and sinless before men, but He was also perfect before His Holy Father. Yes, *God . . . in Christ (2 Corinthians 5:19)* went to the Cross *as a lamb unblemished and spotless (1 Peter 1:19),* and the substitutionary death of Christ for sinners was volunteered by God's heart of love.

The thieves had to die, but certainly the Lord Jesus did not. Earlier, when speaking to His critics, Jesus affirmed: *I lay down My life that I may take it again. No one has taken it away from Me, but . . . I have authority to lay it down, and I have authority to take it up again*

(John 10:17,18). And when explaining to His disciples the extent to which His love would soon go, He said: *Greater love has no one than this, that one lay down his life for his friends (John 15:13).*

It was after the death and resurrection of the Lord Jesus that the Apostle Paul further emphasized: *God was in Christ* and that *He* [God] *made Him* [Christ] *who knew no sin to be sin on our behalf, that we might become the righteousness of God in Him (2 Corinthians 5:21)*. Centuries later, the wonderful truth of Christ's substitutionary death for our sin was meaningfully expressed in these words:

> You are my Righteousness,
> I was Your sin,
> You have taken what was mine
> And given me what was Yours,
> You became what You were not
> That I might become what I was not.

A Grain of Wheat

Being very conscious of His impending death, the Lord Jesus opened His heart to His disciples and said:

> *Now My soul has become troubled; and what shall I say, 'Father, save Me from this hour'? But for this purpose I came to this hour. Father, glorify Thy name.* To this whole-hearted commitment to the glory of God, His Father tenderly responded: *I have both glorified it, and will glorify it again (John 12:27,28).*

But you may be wondering how could the Father be glorified at such a gory scene as that of a Roman crucifixion?

Before the Lord Jesus prayed to the Father, He had already reminded His disciples that it is necessary for a germinal seed to die before there can be an harvest.

> *Truly, truly, I say unto you, unless a grain of wheat falls into the earth and dies, it remains by itself alone; but if it dies, it bears much fruit (John 12:24).*

As a sinless Man, death had no claim upon Jesus. But, He choose to die; die a cruel death as a substitute for your sin and mine. And in this way He would reap an eternal harvest of redeemed people. So the Lord Jesus both tells of His plan, and to every true beliver he also gives His promise.

> [His plan] *I came forth from the Father, and have come into the world; I am leaving the world again, and going to the Father.* [His promise] *I will come again, and receive you to Myself; that where I am, there you may be also (John 16:28; 14:3).*

This is wonderful, but incredible as it may seem, in spite of the Savior's amazing love for them, some people will still choose to reject the forgiveness He offers. Others will remain passive and neutral about His death. However, whether people actively reject the Savior, or whether they passively ignore Him, the result will be the same—separation for ever from the only source of eternal life; eternal light and eternal love. This terrible condition has been described in these words.

> Dying you will die,
> Will die so great a death,
> Will die eternally,
> Be ever dying, yet never dead.

However, the Lord Jesus died not only to get you out of hell and into heaven, but also to get God out of heaven and into you!

No, eternal life is not only the assurance of my future in heaven. The Bible also assures the true beliver that eternal life is a glorious, present, living reality.

> *God has given us eternal life, and this life is in His Son. He who has the Son has the life; he who does not have the Son of God does not have the life . . . (1 John 5:11,12).*

Eternal Life is in a Person—the Lord Jesus Christ. And when He takes His abode in the human heart, at that very moment eternal life begins.

Enormous Cost

At the cross of Christ; the holiness of God, the justice of God and the love of God all met in one supreme act of sacrifice. There, His holiness was vindicated; His justice was satisfied; and there, God's love embraced sinful people such as you and me. But the cost to Him was enormous.

In his daily devotional book *My Utmost for His Highest,* Oswald Chambers issued this salutary warning:

> Beware of the pleasant view of the Fatherhood of God which says, 'God is so kind and loving that of course He will forgive us.' That sentiment has no place in the New Testament whatsoever. The only ground on which God can forgive sin and reinstate us in His favour is through the Cross of Christ, and in no other way. Even if we understand this to be true, it is still possible to take the forgiveness of sin with the simplicity of faith and then forget at what enormous cost to God it was made ours.

Even though we previously mentioned the selfless act of Willie Holt, there is really no human parallel to the suffering God endured at Calvary as an illustration to match His love for us. And through the Spirit-breathed Word we call the Holy Bible, God Himself draws His own curtain aside to give us a fuller glimpse of such sacrificing love. Even then, the magnitude of His love far surpasses the capacity of our limited understanding. However, by reflecting on such an astonishing act of love, we can begin to appreciate a little of the length, breadth, height and the depth of the love of God.

When Jesus died on the Cross He suffered for our sins in a three-fold way.

On the Cross the body of Jesus was racked with

agony; on the Cross His love was stretched to the ultimate; and even more traumatic, on the Cross Jesus was cut off from the light and the glory and the peace that He had forever enjoyed in His oneness with the Father. Yes, the sufferings that Jesus endured are really beyond our human comprehension.

However, as we reflect upon His physical suffering, His emotional suffering and especially upon His spiritual suffering we will appreciate in a new way the measure of His love for sinful people.

Physical Suffering: It is really quite impossible to equate the destruction of a priceless Rembrandt painting with the mutilation of a piece of soiled paper. Even more so, the death of the perfect man, Christ Jesus, can never be equated or even compared adequately to the death of any other human being.

In the Old Testament we find a prophecy that accurately predicted the physical disfigurement that Jesus would later endure. There we are told that His appearance would be *marred more than any man (Isaiah 52:14)*. However, the English translation of this phrase does not convey the full force of the original Hebrew text. In that statement God explained that His beloved Son would be so brutalized that He would no longer resemble a human being. Such a mutilation of Christ's physical form was prophesied by Jesus Himself:

> *Behold, we go up to Jerusalem; and the Son of man shall be delivered unto the chief priests, and unto the scribes; and they shall condemn Him to*

*death, and shall deliver Him to the Gentiles. And
they shall MOCK Him, and shall SCOURGE Him,
and shall SPIT upon Him, and shall KILL Him . . .
(Mark 10:33,34 KJ).*

And this is exactly what happened! Later Mark
described what eyewitnesses had seen: *first they **smote
Him**, then they **did spit upon** Him, after that they
mocked Him, and finally they **crucified Him** (Mark
15:19,20 KJ).*

The Roman scourge that lacerated the Savior's
body was made of leather thongs, weighted with sharp
pieces of bone or lead. These cruelly tore His flesh on
both His back and His breast. That is why it is prophesied in the Psalm that the Messiah would say: . . .
*they pierced my hands and my feet. I may count all my
bones; they look and stare upon me (Psalm 22:16,17
NS).* Yes, the Lord Jesus—perfect in every way—went
to a painful and agonizing death. The callous physical
mutilation that He suffered literally dehumanized His
physical appearance.

Does that better help you understand how much
God loves you?

Emotional Suffering: Though the physical suffering
of the crucified Lord Jesus is beyond our human comprehension, that was only a part of His real suffering.
His physical pain only touched the surface of His deep
agony.

On the Cross Jesus also experienced great emotional anguish. John recorded for us the events of those
dreadful hours:

But coming to Jesus, when they (the Roman soldiers) *saw that He was already dead, they did not break His legs; but one of the soldiers pierced His side with a spear, and immediately there came out blood and water (John 19:33,34).*

I have heard medical authorities express their belief that the presence of both blood and water indicated that Jesus died of a broken heart. Some heart specialists explain this phenomenon further and suggest that, when the heart of Jesus actually broke, His blood effused into the enlarged surrounding sac of the pericardium. This would explain the fact that, as the soldier pierced the Savior's side, there came out both blood and water. In Psalm sixty-nine, among other precise prophecies about Christ's death, we read of a prophetic fore-shadowing of His heart-rending trauma: *Reproach hath broken my heart; and I am full of heaviness . . . (Psalm 69:20 KJ).* Yes, the indescribable emotional suffering of Jesus literally broke His loving heart.

When across His heart of love there surged the total aggregate of the suffering of the human race; and when upon His spotless soul—the soul of Him who was separate from sinners *(Hebrews 7:26)*—there rolled the unthinkable, unprintable filthiness of hell itself, the Lord Jesus died of a broken heart.

Does that better help you understand how much God loves you?

Spiritual Suffering: Most people can more readily understand the physical and emotional suffering of the Lord Jesus than they can His spiritual agony. Yet, surely, the greatest suffering that Jesus endured was when His eternal fellowship with the Father and the Holy Spirit was broken.

For three hours of desolate darkness—from 12 noon to 3 pm—Jesus was forsaken by God the Father and God the Holy Spirit. During that time, Jesus—God the Son—cried with a loud voice: *"My God, My God, why have You forsaken Me?"* (Mt 27:46).

On that startling day, the eternal tri-unity of God's oneness (which had eternally embraced indescribable light) was severed. Severed by your sin and mine. Consequently, when Jesus hung on the Cross, God could not co-exist with the sin that, in His sinless body He bore, because God *"made Him who knew no sin to be sin on our behalf…"* (2 Corinthians 5:21).

Therefore, it is not surprising that, when Jesus died, this wicked world was shadowed in eerie darkness for three solemn hours.

> Well might the sun in darkness hide
> And shut his glories in,
> When Christ, the mighty Maker, died
> For man the creature's sin.
>
> *Isaac Watts (1674–1748)*

"God is light, and in Him is no darkness at all" (1 John 1:5 KJ). The light of God's holiness, and the darkness of man's sinfulness could never co-exist. Just as darkness will disappear when you turn on a light, so darkness will prevail when you turn the light off. It was darkness that prevailed when Jesus bore the sin of lost humanity.

Sadly, this spiritual darkness will also be the eternal state of every person who turns from the light of God's redeeming love. Darkness that is thicker than midnight; lonelier than solitary confinement, and longer than time itself. For: *"This is the condemnation, that light is come into the world, and men loved darkness rather than light, because their deeds were evil" (John 3:19 KJ).* To turn from Jesus will result in spiritual darkness and death—spiritual death and eternal death. To turn to Jesus will result in life—spiritual life and eternal life.

The Victor's Cry

The good news is, that as those three desolate hours of darkness drew to their conclusion, Jesus did not sorrowfully bemoan "I am finished." Certainly not! Love's redeeming work had been accomplished. So now he triumphantly proclaimed *"It is finished"* *(John 19:30).*

The price for your sin and mine has been paid in full. Finished!

Then, having finished His redemptive work, the fellowship of light that the Lord Jesus had forever enjoyed in the triune Godhead was eternally restored *(John 17:5).* Now there is nothing left for you or for me to do to pay for sin. And there is absolutely nothing Satan can do to nullify the completed work of Jesus on your behalf. The sting of Satan, the viper, has been de-fanged.

Death Conquers The Prince of Death

The reason that God clothed Himself with 'flesh and blood' was not only that He might die for your sin and mine, but also that: *Through death he might destroy him that had the power of death, that is, the devil (Hebrews 2:14 KJ).*

Just as David used Goliath's own sword to destroy the stunned Goliath, so Jesus took Satan's own weapon—death—and used it to totally defeat him. Jesus is the true emancipator of man—men and women. He is God's deliverer—the only One who is able to set people free from the eternal death and spiritual bondage—the bondage that Satan had purposed for every person, in his own rebellion against God who created mankind in His own image.

It was in His human body of real flesh and real bones that Jesus defeated Satan, conquered death and rose from the grave. Then we read of His ascent to Heaven, *where Jesus has entered as a forerunner for us (Hebrews 6:20).* For the first time man—a **guiltless, sinless, perfect Man**—had entered Heaven. Because of His death on the cross He has now opened the way for others to follow.

In his day, Charles Wesley was convinced that God really did love him when he wrote "Amazing love: how can it be; that Thou, my God; should die for me?"

But Now is Christ Risen!

"But the fact is that Christ (the Messiah) has been raised from the dead, and become the firstfruits of those who have fallen asleep [in death]. For since [it was] through a man that death [came into the world, it is] also through a Man that the resurrection of the dead [has come]" (1 Corinthians 15:20-21 AMP).

The late Dr. Sangster was one of the most gifted orators that I have ever heard. He delighted to use his silver tongue to speak well of His Lord and Savior Jesus Christ. Ironically, before he died, Dr. Sangster was totally unable to speak because of the cancer in his mouth. Just before going to Heaven, he gestured to his daughter to pass a pencil and paper. That Easter Sunday morning he wrote: "Better to have no tongue and a burning desire to shout 'Christ is risen,' than to have a tongue with no desire to shout!"

When the Apostle Paul appeared before king Agrippa to defend himself against false accusations, he drew their attention both to the suffering and to the resurrection of Christ: *"That Christ should suffer,"* he said *"and that He should be **the first that should rise from the dead**, and should show light unto the people…" (Acts 26:23 AMP).*

However, before the resurrection of the Lord Jesus Christ, in the New Testament it is recorded that other people had been physically raised from the dead. There was Lazarus and the daughter of Jairus as well as the son of the widow of Nain. Though Jesus had miraculously restored these people to physical life they all died again within a few years. However, that is not so with the Lord Jesus Christ. Today, He is not only physically alive, but also spiritually and eternally alive. He was indeed the first that should rise from the dead!

How could a tomb of death and decay imprison the Creator of life? Because the Lord Jesus Christ is the Creator God, He brought life out of nothing. Because, as perfect Man, Jesus is the Savior God He brought life out of the grave and pioneered the way to Heaven for every person who would receive Him, by faith. To them it is promised:

> *"But God, being rich in mercy, because of His great love with which he loved us, even when we were dead in our transgressions, made us alive together with Christ (by grace you have been saved), and raised us up with Him, and seated us with Him in the heavenly places, in Christ Jesus" (Ephesians 2:4-6).*

Writing to believers in the city of Corinth, the Apostle Paul reminded them that they had been saved from the consequences of their sin because they had *received* (adhered to; trusted in and rested upon) that *Christ died for our sins according to the Scriptures, and that He was buried, **and** that He was raised on the third day according to the Scriptures (1 Corinthians 15:3,4).* Today, every true believer rests upon the glorious fact that "Christ died for my sins; and rose again, and gives me new life in Him."

From Day One to Day Three

Now, you may be wondering, "what happened to the Lord Jesus Christ between the time He was crucified and the time He rose from the grave three days later?" Anticipating such a question, God revealed the answer:

What does 'he ascended' mean except that he also descended to the lower, earthly regions? He who descended is the very one who ascended higher than all the heavens, in order to fill the whole universe (Ephesians 4:9,10 NIV).

Yes, the Bible tells us that before ascending to Heaven, the Lord Jesus Christ actually descended to *the lower regions*. After that He ascended to Heaven leading Old Testament saints (who had died believing) in the train of His triumph. Today, every true believer is happily assured that the door of death is really his gateway to glory. Miraculously, Christ Himself has triumphed over both physical and spiritual death on our behalf.

O death, where is thy sting? O grave, where is thy victory? The sting of death is sin; and the strength of sin is the law. But thanks be to God, who giveth us the victory through our Lord Jesus Christ (1 Corinthians 15:55-57 NS).

Appendage—The Bequest of His Love

It is wonderful to know that the Lord Jesus has pioneered the way to Heaven and that now we can follow in the train of His triumph.

It is equally wonderful to know that before His death, in love for His own, Jesus promised that after His ascension to Heaven He would send the Holy Spirit to believers on earth.

To His disciples He said:

He who believes in Me, as the Scripture said, "From his innermost being shall flow rivers of living water." But this He spoke of the Spirit, whom those who believed in Him were to receive; for the Spirit was not yet given, because Jesus was not yet glorified. (John 7:38-39)

But now I am going to Him who sent Me . . . And I will ask the Father, and He will give you another Helper . . . the Spirit of truth . . . it is to your advantage that I go away; for if I do not go away, the Helper shall not come to you; but if I go, I will send Him to you . . . He shall glorify Me (John 16:5;14:16,17;16:7,14).

We have already noticed how God was glorified in the death of His Son. Now you may ask another question: "How can Jesus be glorified by sending the Holy Spirit to you and me?"

This question is partly answered by the fact that Jesus is glorified in the life of each believer through whom the love of God is flowing. We read: *the love of God has been poured out within our hearts through the Holy Spirit who was given to us (Romans 5:5).* God's indwelling love—made real by the Holy Spirit—far transcends the loftiest pinnacle of human attraction or affection. As by faith you respond to His finished work at the Cross, the Lord Jesus, in the Person of the Holy Spirit, will begin to love other people through you. Marvelous!

To believe that Christ died for your sins, and then to give thanks in your heart for that fact, is for you to enjoy the personal assurance of God's forgiveness and saving love.

Then, to make your life available to the indwelling presence of the Lord Jesus Christ is for you to become the vehicle of His love to a loveless world.

A German theologian, famous for his scholarship, was once asked the question: "What is your most profound thought about God?" Astonishingly he replied in the words of a children's chorus: "Jesus loves me; this I know, for the Bible tells me so."

Yes, God truly loves me! and yes, God TRULY does love you!

> O, the love that drew salvation's plan,
> O, the grace that brought it down to man,
> O, the mighty gulf that God did span,
> At Calvary!
> Mercy there was great, and grace was free,
> Pardon there was multiplied to me,

There my burdened soul found liberty,
At Calvary.

A Letter from Iraq

"I was in a Muslim (Scheltey) house. My family taught me how to pray and fast as a Muslim. I dressed like Muslim women, covering my face so no man would sin if he looked in my face.

"Because of all this, I had a lot of time with nothing to do. Therefore I used my empty time listening to many radio programs and heard many Bible messages. One day I saw my sister-in-law with some nice stickers with pretty colors. Then I wrote my first letter under my sister-in-law's address. Your reply contained the book Your Quest for God.

"I tried to understand what it meant to quest for God... In Chapter 7 there is a question, 'Does God really love me?' In particular I stopped at the paragraph which says: 'God shows His love for you by what He did for you on the Cross. When you understand the meaning of the Cross you do not need any further proof that God loves you.'

"I read this chapter more than 100 times. Then I began to understand without any doubt that the Cross was the only way for me."

– Report submitted by Trans World Radio

Pause to Consider

1. What is the best way to prove you love somebody?

   Is it by what you say?

   Is it by what you do?

2. How did God prove His love for you?

3. How will you personally respond to God's love?

In the electronic atmosphere of the operation room, every surgeon learns to identify blood with life. The two are inseparable: you lose one, you lose both.

DR. PAUL BRAND

Chapter 8

Where can I find life?

*I*t was fast approaching the midnight hour. In the middle of a tedious eighteen hour railway journey, my wife and I were with hundreds of fellow-travelers at Gare St. Lazare railway station in Paris. We all waited patiently for the railway official to open the ticket barrier and let us proceed to our train.

The vast majority of those around us were young people. As Dorothy and I mingled among them, it seemed that every country in Europe was represented in the throng. Some of the fellows and girls tried to catch a nap, using their haversack as a poor substitute for a comfortable pillow. While they sprawled on the stone paving, their friends stood guard and munched a sandwich or sipped a bottle of water.

During our wait, we chatted and laughed with a number of these young people. In spite of their youthful excitement, when their facade was down, most of them were conscious that they had not yet found that illusive 'life' for which they were searching. Before long, our conversation turned to the Person who was travelling with Dorothy and me—the Lord Jesus Christ!

As we talked, some of these restless and adventuresome young people opened up and shared with us their desire to find 'real' life. Some hoped it would be in the next city; some thought it might be in the next friendship; others unabashedly believed they would expand their life experience in the next drug fix or booze party. Of great concern to some was the fear of being infected with a deadly disease.

In remote African villages, they call this feared plague 'the thin man's disease.' In medical parlance it is diagnosed as HIV positive. When fully developed in a man, woman, boy or girl, it is known as AIDS. The dreaded news of having contracted this disease is always the same: instant and utter devastation! Around the world, people know that the terrible affliction of AIDS is a 'blood disease.' Whereas the blood stream should be a cleansing river of life, it has become a contaminated river of death.

I have to admit, however, that though blood is a vital life-giving stream, to me the sight of blood has always been repulsive. In fact, in a bold effort to overcome my phobia, I once accepted an invitation to view a surgical operation from an observation tower at a hospital in London. As the scalpel made its incision into the patient's skin, once again I nearly fainted. My doctor friend, who noticed that I was bathed in perspiration and ashen-white, suggested that I step out of the viewing room. I needed no further persuasion!

But, regardless of a person's reaction to the sight of blood, life and health can be restored to a person who is seriously hemorrhaging by giving a blood-transfusion. Today, because of the marvels of modern science, blood taken from the veins of a healthy individual can later be introduced as a life-giving river into the veins of a dying or seriously ill patient.

Long before medical research began to unfold the marvels and mysteries of blood, God Himself declared: *For the life of the flesh is in the blood . . . (Leviticus 17:11).* Dr. Paul Brand succinctly agrees that blood contains the essence of life: "In the electronic atmosphere of the operation room, every surgeon learns to identify blood with life. The two are inseparable: you lose one, you lose both."

However, many people are not aware that, although blood contaminations such as the HIV infection are selective depending upon exposure, there is another 'disease' that is universal. Because God *hath made of one blood all nations of men for to dwell on all the face of the earth (Acts 17:26 KJ);* this deathly contamination has afflicted the whole human race. In the Bible, its source is traced back to Adam, the progenitor of all successive generations.

When: *the first man, Adam, (1 Corinthians 15:45)* sinned, all subsequent generations, of whatever color of skin, place of residence or station in life, came under the sentence of death. The Bible clearly states: . . . *in Adam all die . . . (1 Corinthians 15:22).* Yes, as with AIDS death is carried to the body through contaminated blood, so too this contamination caused by sin has been passed on from generation to generation. If this had not been so, people would have gone straight to Heaven without passing through the valley of physical disease and death. But such is not the case.

Thank God, however, that when Jesus was born, a life-giving stream of Blood was introduced into the human race. This is how it happened. The angel Gabriel told Mary that she was to conceive and bear a Son and that His name would be called Jesus. Gabriel also explained to this chaste, unmarried virgin how her conception would occur.

The Holy Spirit will come upon you, and the power of the Most High will overshadow you; and for that reason the holy offspring shall be called the Son of God (Luke 1:35).

A miracle took place when the seed of the woman was fertilized by the Seed of the Holy Spirit. In this dramatic event the Life of God was introduced to the human race. Then, as the babe began to grow in the womb of Mary, and blood circulated in the embryo, His precious Blood was unadulterated and uncontaminated. Yes, the Blood of the Lord Jesus was Life itself!*

Human blood is an incredibly complex substance. Even today, those involved in medical research continue to discover more of the life-giving secrets of this miraculous fluid. In simple terms, some of the functions of blood in the human body can be described as: body-cleansing, life-supplying and disease-repelling. Marvelous as this may be, it is even more wonderful to know that God has made available to you and me a Blood-stream that has similar yet far more miraculous purposes. And that Blood is there for all those who seek 'real' life. For the sinner, the Blood of Jesus is God's cleansing agent from sin. For the spiritually dead, His precious Blood transfuses Life with a capital 'L'. For the spiritually alive, the Blood of Jesus is God's protecting agent from the attacks of Satan. Of this precious Blood we read: *Knowing that you were not redeemed with perishable things like silver or gold from your futile way of life inherited from your forefathers, but with precious blood, as of a lamb unblemished and spotless, the blood of Christ* (1 Peter 1:18,19).

The Blood: Its Cleansing Power

A while back, the news media reported that a greedy transport firm had compromised hygienic

---

* In his book: The Chemistry of the blood, M.R. DeHaan, M.D., quotes several recognized physiological, obstetric and nursing publications and concludes: "The mother provides the fetus (the unborn developing infant) with nutritive elements for the building of that little body in the secret of her womb, but all the blood which forms in it is formed in the embryo itself. From the time of conception to the time of birth not one single drop of blood ever passes from the mother to the child.' However, commenting on DeHaan's view, Dr. Robert E. Coleman in his book: Written in Blood states: 'Without trying to discredit this position, [DeHaan's view that the blood of the human body is formed in the fetus itself by the introduction of the male sperm, and therefore has no direct contact with the mother's body] I think it is only fair to note that other medical doctors seriously question its validity. However, regardless of the biological nature of the situation, I see no reason why it should be an issue. The fact that Jesus was conceived by God would itself rule out the hereditary transmission of sin when considering the Biblical significance of the Blood of Jesus.'

requirements. To increase their profit, this firm had utilized a tank truck to carry poisonous products in one direction and then, unofficially, used the same tank to carry a fluid food product on the return journey. This resulted in many people becoming critically ill.

However, in the human body, God has made a miraculous transport system that both carries food to the cells and at the same time scavenges the refuse. And because of God's perfect creation, there is no cross-contamination within the bloodstream. Amazingly, no cell in the human body is more than a hair's breadth from a blood capillary. If poisonous products were not eliminated from these cells, the inevitable result would be disease and death.

And that is exactly what God has described when He explained His method of removing the contaminating presence of sin from our lives. Such cleansing is only through the precious Blood of Jesus: *but if we walk in the light as He Himself is in the light, we have fellowship with one another, and the blood of Jesus His Son cleanses us from all sin (1 John 1:7).* Furthermore, God has said that there is no other way that our sins can be forgiven, for *without shedding of blood there is no forgiveness (Hebrews 9:22).*

The Blood: Its Life-Giving Power
Another function of the blood is to carry the needed water and nourishment throughout the body to sustain life. If blood fails to reach the cells and tissues of the body, those body structures promptly die. Thus the body dies when the blood ceases to circulate.

Obviously, the life is in the blood.

Realizing this, we are reminded of the words of the Lord Jesus that so startled His disciples when He spoke of His own Blood. He emphatically said:

Unless you eat the flesh of the Son of Man and drink His blood, you have no life in yourselves. He who eats My flesh and drinks My blood has eternal life; and I will raise him up on the last day. For My flesh is true food, and My blood is true drink (John 6:53-55).

However, Jesus went on to clarify His real meaning. He said: . . . *he who eats My flesh and drinks My blood abides in Me, and I in him (John 6:56).* What a joy it is to understand the true source of spiritual life! The Blood of Jesus was shed to redeem sinners from their sin. And because of His shed Blood we can now partake of His shared life. The Lord Jesus explained the true meaning of drinking His Blood when He said—'I in him'! Marvelous!

Having personally experienced the resurrection power of Christ's indwelling presence, believers can triumphantly testify: "the risen Christ now lives in me!" For such people, the partaking of bread and wine at a communion service is a simple and symbolic act of thanksgiving and testimony.*

---

* Sadly, there are millions of people who still persist in believing that the bread and the wine served at certain 'Eucharists' are literally changed into Christ's physical flesh and blood. What our Lord intended to be understood as a symbol of His indwelling life has tragically been understood as a literal and physical fact.

The germinal life-giving power of the precious Blood of Jesus is miraculously conveyed to the life of the believer by the power of the Holy Spirit when he is born from above. Yes, basic to every person's search for life is the need of a life-giving 'Blood transfusion.'

The Blood: Its Protecting Power

There is yet another miracle function of the human blood. Not only is the blood life-cleansing and life-giving but it is also life-protecting.

Fear spread around the world when the bubonic plague was diagnosed in India. Inter-continental jet aircraft which originated in that country were fumigated and, in some cases, the passengers were temporarily quarantined for medical examination. Lest this killer disease should spread to other countries, a temporary embargo was then placed on all subsequent flights leaving India.

Even without the threat of bubonic plague there is always a constant bombardment of the human body by alien and life-threatening germs. But the blood has a marvelous mechanism of counterattack. It carries in its life-defending stream antitoxins and other specific substances which defend the system against bacterial invasion. When such an invasion occurs the white blood cells (primarily there for defensive purposes) dramatically increase in number and jump into a defensive mode.

How wonderful to know that the Blood of the Lord Jesus Christ, much like the marvelous power of human blood, also has a life-protecting ministry. It is the Blood of Jesus Christ that protects the believer from the constant bombardment of Satanic forces. In the prophecy about the end-time battle between Satan and God's people, we read: *And they overcame him because of the blood of the Lamb and because of the word of their testimony, and they did not love their life even to death (Revelation 12:11).* You also can overcome the foul advances of the devil by the protecting power of the precious Blood of Jesus.

This victory of Jesus over Satan was prophesied immediately following the devil's seduction of Adam and Eve. Then, the Lord God promised that it would be the seed of the woman who would cause his doom. *And I will put enmity . . . between your seed and her seed; he shall bruise you on the head, and you shall bruise him on the heel (Genesis 3:15).* The seed of the woman would crush Satan's head but not before that serpent had fanged Messiah's heel. Yes, it was the Lord Jesus Christ Himself, the seed of the woman, who shed His precious Blood so that:

> *Through death He might destroy him that had the power of death, that is, the devil (Hebrews 2:14 KJ).*

Unlike the illusion-chasing students we met at Gare St. Lazare station in Paris, many others have discovered the source of real life.

Some time ago, Dorothy and I met with a hundred Ugandans who were assured that they had found true life. In the precious Blood of the Lord Jesus Christ they had discovered a heartcleansing, life-giving and devil-resisting power. They could truly attest that, for them, the old things had passed away and that everything had become new.

Although it was against the advice of Embassy officials in Kenya who had warned us of impending danger, my wife and I, urged by the Spirit of God, proceeded to Uganda. God had planned the timing of our protracted seminar with Ugandan pastors and their wives. As we later discovered, He had also pre-planned our return flight. (It so happened that ours was the last plane to leave Entebbe before yet another military coup.)

Immediately upon our arrival at the airport, we sensed an atmosphere of tension and fear. The confusion and dirt we encountered were indescribable. One of the few cars in the region had been made available for us to drive from the airport on a road that was still pitted with bomb holes. After a short distance we were apprehended at gunpoint by unruly soldiers. We didn't know whether they were government soldiers, anti-government soldiers or just thugs dressed in soldiers' uniforms. Remarkably, they soon recognized our driver as belonging to their own tribe so they reluctantly allowed us to proceed without our being robbed or hurt in any way.

Upon arriving at our destination, my wife and I found the meeting place for our seminars to be a dark and dirty structure in the middle of a fear-ridden community. When the pastors and their wives arrived, however, we soon forgot these surroundings. It was the Lord Himself who graced us with an overwhelming sense of His glory and His presence. Those meetings in Uganda will forever be etched in our memory as a mountain-top experience of our meeting with the Living God.

With rapt attention, the pastors and their wives sat on uncomfortable benches for eight hours a day to hear Dorothy and me share God's truth from the Bible. As I taught, my wife wrote my outlines on an old blackboard to help the listeners take notes on treasured scraps of paper. Suddenly, there was a scuffle at the door. Though one of the drunken men with his rifle had been apprehended at the entrance, his partner had pushed his way through the crowd, brandishing his rifle as he pointed it at Dorothy's heart.

"Let's all pray that this dear man will come to know Jesus," she quietly said.

After moments which, to me, had seemed like an eternity, my interpreter turned to me with absolute astonishment: "I can't believe what that drunken soldier has said—he just said, 'I want to know this woman's God.'"

Even as the translator spoke, I saw a sight I will never forget. Whatever the cause—whether it was an angel compelling the intruder to his knees, whether it was the awesome sense of God's holiness and power which had prevailed in our meetings becoming too much for the drunken soldier, or whether it was a voluntary act of humility prompting him to openly express his heart's deep need—I know not. What I do know is that at that precise moment the barrel of the rifle slowly slipped downward and then the intended weapon of destruction dropped to the ground as the soldier fell to his knees.

This was no moment for a well-thought-out after-meeting of instruction! And Dorothy knew it. "Pray this prayer after me," she said. Then, step by step she led this poor deluded and needy soul to the foot of the Cross—to the Savior of sinful men—where he found the source of all true life through the Blood of Jesus.

Why do I share this experience now? Simply because of what happened next in that memorable meeting.

In our gathering there were many men who might have had every reason to fear and even hate the intruder who had so violently made his way into our meeting. There were those among us whose lives had recently been threatened. One pastor present had even had his fingers blown off by such a soldier during an aborted attempt to kill him. But because they knew and loved the Lord Jesus in a personal way, these very men gathered around him to embrace him and pray for their new brother in Christ.

Then, without any musical accompaniment, but in glorious African harmony, they burst into song. My heart is still filled with awe as I reflect upon the words sung:

> Oh, the Blood of Jesus,
> Oh, the Blood of Jesus,
> Oh, the Blood of Jesus
> That cleanses me from sin.

If only our world leaders could have been with us that day. Surely they, too, would have witnessed God's only solution to inter-tribal, inter-racial and international conflict:

> *And through Him to reconcile all things to Himself, having made peace through the blood of His cross (Colossians 1:20) . . . And you, that were once alienated and enemies in your mind by wicked works, yet now has He reconciled . . . (Colossians 1:21 KJ).*

Yes, only those who have been brought into a right relationship with God, *"by His* [Christ's] *blood . . . shall be saved from the wrath of God through Him. . . . much more, having been reconciled, we shall be saved by His life." (Romans 5:9-10).*

Pause to Consider

1. Do you really desire 'life' with a capital 'L'? This is the life that the Lord Jesus described when He said: *I came that they might have life, and might have it abundantly (John 10:10).*

2. According to the Bible, where in the human body is life to be found? (Read Leviticus 17:11).

3. What is the eternal significance of the precious Blood of the Lord Jesus?

   Are you trusting in its cleansing power?

   Are you trusting in its life-giving power?

   Are you trusting in its protecting power?

   The Lord Jesus said: *I am the resurrection, and the life; he who believes in Me, shall live even if he dies, and everyone who lives and believes in Me shall never die (John 11:25,26).*

The perfection of an artist's painting, the radiance of a human face, the grandeur of a landscape—surely none of these can be adequately described by sound. Sight is needed.

Chapter 9

How can I become part of God's family?

*D*uring the early 1940's, medical science made great progress in the field of eye surgery. So much so, in fact, that it had become possible to transplant healthy corneas from the eyes of someone who had just died into the eyes of a blind person. Dr. Sangster told us about his witnessing the results of the first successful cornea transplant.

Long before sunrise, Dr. Sangster accompanied two people to the beautiful Surrey Downs in England. One was a lady who had been born blind; the other was her eye surgeon. Layers of bandages had protected the patient's eyes from any light on the days following her operation. Gradually these had been peeled off. Already she had become aware of a new sensitivity to light and was very excited. And now before sunrise, the last remaining bandage was removed from the eyes of this lady who had never seen.

That day the sunrise could not have been more glorious as the morning sun peeped over the horizon. Shadows grew shorter and green leaves silhouetted their delicate beauty on a backdrop of morning splendor. Birds busily hopped over the dew-drenched turf in search of their breakfast. The whole scene presented exquisite entertainment for a lady who could see for the first time in her life. With tears streaming down her cheeks, she exclaimed: "Oh, you've tried to describe it to me but I never imagined that anything could be so wonderful!" She then sat in silent awe before the splendor of God's creation.

How would you try to describe the color of red to a person who has never seen? Or the drama of a sunset to a person whose eyes have never responded to light? It would surely be impossible. Words that describe visual beauty can have little meaning when they fall on the ears of a hearer who has no visual frame of reference. The perfection of an artist's painting, the radiance of a human face, the grandeur of a landscape—surely none of these can be adequately described by sound. Sight is needed.

The same difficulty is encountered when a believer tries to convey spiritual beauty to a non-believer. Once while talking to a medical student who was studying for his final exams at Guy's Hospital in London, I tried to explain the wonder of God's love. "I just can't see it," he replied. I understood, but pursued the conversation a little further: "No, I don't suspect you can, because you are like a man who is living in a dark room. I know what that is like; I have lived in spiritual darkness myself, but now I am outside where the sun of God's love is shining. David," I said, "if you are to understand the love of God, you must come out of that darkened room and into His sunlight." That day David knelt to ask the Lord Jesus to forgive his sin and to enter his life. I will never forget what he said as he rose from his knees: "I never thought it could be as wonderful as this!"

Just as physical sight conveys the beauty of God's creation to human experience, so spiritual sight relays the reality of God's presence, power and love to the human soul.

After He had ascended to Heaven, the Lord Jesus, speaking through the Apostle John, gave a startling diagnosis concerning the spiritual condition of the people in the city of Laodicea. To them He said: *You . . . do not know that you are . . . blind (Revelation 3:17 NKJV)*. Can you imagine a blind person who is not aware of his sad state? After the diagnosis of spiritual blindness, the Lord Jesus went on to prescribe His remedy. *Anoint your eyes with eye salve that you may see (Revelation 3:18 NKJV)*. And how important that prescription is! Spiritual blindness requires spiritual eye surgery, which is the work of the Holy Spirit.

The first time you were born it was a physical birth. But that did not give you spiritual sight and understanding. If you are to find your way out of spiritual darkness into the *light of the knowledge of the glory of*

God (2 Corinthians 4:6), you need to be born a second time. Jesus said to Nicodemus:

> *That which is born of the flesh is flesh; and that which is born of the Spirit is spirit. Do not marvel that I said to you, 'You must be born again' (John 3:6,7), . . . unless one is born again, he cannot see the kingdom of God (John 3:3).*

So if you are to see the kingdom of God, you too need to be born again.

Like every other human being, you were born with a God-shaped vacuum in your life that cries out to be filled. This spiritual emptiness can only be satisfied by the incoming and indwelling presence of the Risen Christ. When you receive Him into your life as your Savior, the purpose and necessity of His death will be brought to fruition in your life. He did not die just to forgive you your sins; He died so that your heart could be made a spiritually clean place for Him to reside. And it is necessary that your sins be forgiven before He can come to live in your heart.

While talking to a young African believer, I became aware of his intense burden to share the good news about Christ with the young people of his country. The following week I was to teach the Bible to nearly two hundred pastors so I invited him to join us. Though we were then several hundred miles from where the pastors were to gather, I suggested that he travel by bus over the long, bumpy roads to meet with us. William arrived worn and weary but very happy to be able to learn more about God and His Word. William had not traveled on that overcrowded African bus just to have a ride! The bus trip was obviously his means of getting to the conference. His real purpose was what awaited him at the end of his journey.

Similarly, the Lord Jesus knew that the only way He could ever enter your life in order to fellowship with you and you with Him would be for Him to provide a way for your heart to be cleansed from sin. Although the forgiveness of your sins was necessary, your new life in Christ and your ability to fellowship with God were His ultimate desire for you. Can you be content with anything less? After all, this personal relationship with Christ is the very purpose for which you were created.

To know that Christ lives in your heart is to know here and now that eternal life has already begun. Christ's indwelling presence brings His life to your life.

And the witness is this, that God has given us eternal life, and this life is in His Son. He who has the Son has the life; he who does not have the Son of God does not have the life (1 John 5:11-12).

Thus, it is not surprising that after my friend David asked the Lord Jesus to forgive his sin and to enter his life, he exclaimed: "I never thought it could be as wonderful as this!"

But How?

When people heard Peter preach about the life, the death and the resurrection of Jesus, God gave them a desire to know the Savior. The Holy Spirit did for them what He is doing for you. They listened to Peter tell them that Jesus was Lord ('Kurios'—Yahweh) and the Messiah of God. And this new understanding of who Jesus is produced in them an overwhelming sense of conviction and of their need of salvation. As they reflected on their own rejection of, or indifference to, the Crucified One—to the Savior Himself—the record tells us that they were pierced to the heart, and earnestly asked, *what shall we do? (Acts 2:37).*

Peter's first reply to them was an exhortation to repent. Without repentance, faith is not real faith; it is merely 'make-believe' or 'fantasy.' Saving faith includes both an attitude of trust and a change of attitude.

When in simple trust you thank Jesus for what He did for you when He died on the Cross, your attitude towards God and towards sin has undergone a dramatic change. It is only then that the Holy Spirit performs His spiritual eye surgery and your mind begins to see things from a different perspective. In fact, the meaning of the word repentance is 'a change of mind.' So a genuine new-birth experience involves a basic change of mind regarding God and sin.

Regarding God: Repentance (a change of mind) rejects every false concept of God. I have seen people in Africa who, having struggled mightily with the pull of their old ways and pagan customs, have openly burned their fetishes after having turned to Jesus. I also have friends who have had to resist great social pressures, even having to face threats and danger, when they have turned from religious or social systems that were not true to the God of the Bible. Saving faith must be rooted in the firm conviction that Jesus is Yahweh—the only Savior God.

Regarding sin: When, by faith, you enter into your salvation experience, you will recognize your own sinfulness with sorrow and shame. Your change of mind (repentance) with regard to sin will mean that you no longer try to ignore your sin; you no longer try to excuse your sin; and you no longer hope that your righteousness will save you. Man's *righteous deeds are like a filthy garment* before a Holy God *(Isaiah 64:6)*. But when you turn to Jesus, you will have a desire to turn away from those things in your life that have been displeasing to Him.

Imagine an army corporal on leave from his barracks. One day he receives two letters. One is from a friend; the other is from his Commanding Officer. In the first letter there is an invitation to his friend's wedding, but in the other there is a command from his superior to report for duty. There is certainly a difference between an invitation and a command. An invitation could be politely refused, but a command can only be answered either by obedience or rebellion.

Because God loves you and knows that sin will destroy your life, He does not invite you to repent; He commands you to repent. As Paul concluded his presentation of the gospel to the philosophers and bystanders at the university capital of Greece, he said: *"but now* [God] *commandeth all men everywhere to repent" (Acts 17:30 KJ).* And, "all" includes you.

The miracle is that when you turn from your misconceptions about God and likewise turn away from your personal sin, and in so doing by faith turn to Jesus to acclaim Him as your Savior God, the Holy Spirit will work in your heart *both to will and to do (Philippians 2:13 KJ)* what is right in the eyes of God. Thus, God promises to those who truly repent both the desire to do and the power to perform the will of God. Only then will your life be transformed and reach its God-ordained potential.

As a friend, I urge you to receive the Lord Jesus Christ without delay. Find a quiet spot where you can bow before God in prayer. Of course, if you only repeat words in a parrot-like fashion, they will do nothing for you. The important thing is that you respond in faith to Jesus, who said: *I am the way, and the truth, and the life; no one comes to the Father, but through Me (John 14:6).*

Now you may wish to close your eyes and pray a spontaneous response from your heart, or you may find the following suggested prayer helpful.

My Prayerful Response

Oh God, I have not known You and neither have I loved You. But I thank You that You have both known me and loved me.

I am a sinner, and of myself I can do nothing to earn my salvation. By faith I now turn to You, Lord Jesus, and ask for your forgiveness! I confess that I am a sinner and repent of my sin. Thank you, Lord Jesus, for dying for me and for offering me the cleansing and life-giving power of Your precious Blood. By faith I now place my life under the protection of that precious Blood.

Please come into my heart, Lord Jesus, and take control of my life.

Thank You, Lord Jesus, that by Your Holy Spirit I have been born again. It is wonderful for me to know that by Your risen power I am a child of God and will live with You forever!

And he who believes in Him . . . [trusts in and relies on Him] shall never be disappointed or put to shame (1 Peter 2:6 Amp).

Now, tell somebody what you have just done. Remember Christ lives in you, and He is all the strength you need to be able to speak and live for Him:

. . . If you confess with your mouth Jesus as Lord, and believe in your heart that God raised Him from the dead, you shall be saved; for with the heart man believes, resulting in righteousness, and with the mouth he confesses, resulting in salvation (Romans 10:9-10).

A Letter from Slovakia

"*Dear friends, I have just finished reading the most fascinating book I have ever read in my life,* **Your Quest for God.** *I know I will never be the same again. The Lord Jesus accepted me and I gave my life to Him. I want this joy to belong to every one of my friends and so I kindly ask if I could order two more copies just for lending to others* . . .

"*Thank you for bringing the Gospel and the gift of salvation in Christ into my life* . . . *We never knew that such an excellent book existed.*"

– Report translated and submitted by J.A.

Pause to Consider

1. How can you best express your gratitude for receiving a generous gift?

   Is it by saying: "please give it to me"?

   Is it by saying: "thank you"?

2. Is it your feeling or your faith that gives you assurance that you are a child of God?

   For by grace you have been saved through faith; and that not of yourselves, it is the gift of God (Ephesians 2:8).

3. Does your faith in the Lord Jesus include:

   an element of repentance?

   an element of thanksgiving?

   an attitude of total dependence upon Him?

4. Will you now thank God for saving you and praise the Lord Jesus, not only for what He has done for you, but also for who He is?

There is nothing—no circumstance, no trouble, no testing—that can ever touch me until, first of all, it has gone past God and gone past Christ, right through to me. If it has come that far, it has come with a great purpose, which I may not understand at the moment. But as I refuse to become panicky, as I lift my eyes to His and accept it as coming from the throne of God for some great purpose of blessing to my own heart, no sorrow will ever disturb me, no trial will ever disarm me, no circumstance will cause me to fret—for I shall rest in the joy of what my Lord is. That is the victory of faith!

ALAN REDPATH

Chapter 10

What next?

*S*alvation is absolutely free! There is nothing anybody can do to earn it. The Lord Jesus does it all.

As you sincerely prayed the suggested prayer (or something similar), your faith in Christ has made you a true child of God.

> *But as many as received Him, to them He gave the right to become children of God, even to those who believe in His name (John 1:12).*

Most likely you will now be asking the question, "What next?"

Just before Jesus left His disciples on His mission to conquer death and then to return to Heaven, He said: *Abide in Me, and I in you (John 15:4).* In those words, the Lord Jesus explained the essence of Christian living. From God's point of view, the believer abides in His Son—there to be kept and protected until safely arriving in Heaven. However, from a human perspective, because the risen Lord also abides in true believers, their family, friends and fellow workers will be introduced to a quality of life that can only be explained in terms of the indwelling Christ.

Imagine, if you will, a metal poker in a fire. When you look at it, you could say "the poker is in the fire," but if you look more closely you would observe that the poker itself is red-hot and then it would be quite right for you also to say "the fire is in the poker!" Or, likewise, imagine a cup as it is plunged into a bucket of water. The cup is in the water, but the water is also in the cup!

When you were born again, the Holy Spirit actually baptized (immersed) you into the body of Christ.

Now the Bible assures you that: *your life is hidden with Christ in God (Colossians 3:3).* Yes, because you have been born again, you are now in Christ. Marvelous! Also, when you were born again, the indwelling life of the risen Christ was made a personal and glorious reality by the power of the Holy Spirit. Now, you can rejoice that it is *Christ **in** you, the hope of glory . . . (Colossians 1:27).* And yes, because you have been born again, the risen Christ now lives in you. Wonderful!

Now let us further consider what the Bible actually says about the liberating impact of this twin truth—I am in Christ and Christ is in me.

I am in Christ

For by one Spirit we were all baptized into one body . . . (1 Corinthians 12:13).

Or do you not know that all of us who have been baptised into Christ Jesus have been baptised into

His death? Therefore we have been buried with Him through baptism into death, in order that as Christ was raised from the dead through the glory of the Father, so we too might walk in newness of life (Romans 6:3,4).

For you have died and your life is hidden with Christ in God (Colossians 3:3).

Several years ago I knew a little boy who had leukemia. At that time he was only seven, and he had to go to the doctor every three months for a spinal injection. On one visit the doctor asked Daryl why he did not cry like other boys and girls when the needle penetrated his spine. "Doesn't it hurt?" the doctor asked. "Oh yes, it hurts," replied Daryl, "but, doctor, you don't understand; the needle has to go through the hand of Jesus before it touches me." It is wonderful to know that because you are now in Christ, He is adequate to handle everything that tests and touches your life! That's faith!

Just as you received the Lord Jesus by faith, so it is the same principle of faith that enables you to appropriate the sufficiency of the Lord Jesus Christ to meet every demand of life. In other words, your initial act of faith opened the door for you to adopt a continual attitude of faith. *As you therefore have **received** Christ Jesus the Lord, so **walk** in Him (Colossians 2:6).*

Though you have been born again, God does not expect you to just mimic the life of Jesus. Millions of Christians have been totally frustrated as they have tried to do this and always without success. But God tells us of His wonderful provision for our Christian lives. We have already died in Christ. And being dead in Christ, we are dead to all the demands and condemnation of the law. Therefore, as in the past so now and in the future, we are dead to any hope that self-effort will meet the law's demands. Yes, we are dead to every vestige of confidence in ourselves to live the spiritual life. But, praise God, we are gloriously alive to all the protecting and enabling sufficiency of the risen Lord Jesus Christ!

The problem arises when we try to handle the temptations and pressures of life by ourselves. The new believer will find that all by himself he is just as incapable of living the Christian life after his new birth as he was before. Warning us about this tendency, the Lord Jesus Christ clearly said: . . . *for apart from Me you can do nothing (John 15:5).*

In fact, addressing the foolishness of self-effort, the Apostle Paul actually had blunt words to say to believers in the region of Galatia. To correct their turning away from God's principle of living by faith and faith only, Paul asked a rhetorical question which was designed to lead to a self-evident answer:

> *This is the only thing I want to find out from you: did you receive the Spirit by the works of the Law, or by hearing with faith? Are you so foolish? Having begun by the Spirit, are you now being perfected by the flesh? (Galatians 3:2-3).*

Of course they began their new life in Christ even as you did by an act of faith. And it is only by that same dependent faith that they can hope to: *reign in life through the One, Jesus Christ (Romans 5:17)*.

In Galatia, the vitality of dependent faith had sadly been replaced by the barrenness of legalistic self-effort. But, thank God, if you continue to live in dependence upon your new-found Lord, that sad state of affairs which existed in Galatia need never be your experience.

Christ Lives in Me

*I have been crucified with Christ; and it is no longer I who live, but **Christ lives in me** . . . (Galatians 2:20).*

*And if **Christ is in you**, though the body is dead because of sin, yet the spirit is alive because of righteousness. But if the Spirit of Him who raised Jesus from the dead dwells in you, He who raised Christ Jesus from the dead will also give life to your mortal bodies through His Spirit who indwells you (Romans 8:10-11).*

*To whom God willed to make known what is the riches of the glory of this mystery among the Gentiles, which is **Christ in you,** the hope of glory (Colossians 1:27).*

That Christ may dwell in your hearts through faith . . . (Ephesians 3:17).

You may express your dependent faith upon Christ's indwelling life by saying: "Thank You, Lord

Jesus; You are everything that I am not. I give You permission to be what You are both in me and through me." The astonishing reality of your Christian life is that God has transferred the responsibility for your success to somebody else—the Lord Jesus Christ! Jesus is the only one who is adequate to meet the temptations and opportunities of life you will surely face. It is possible for you to be a 'theologian' without Christ, it is possible for you to be a 'preacher' without Christ, it is possible for you to be a 'missionary' without Christ; but it is impossible for you to be a Christian if Christ does not live in your heart.

Jesus is the only Person who can truly live the Christian life. Now, by His Spirit He has miraculously taken up His residence in your heart. Now He can do through you and for you what you could never do for yourself. He who is pure is your purity in a world of immorality; He who is Victor is your victory in a world of temptation; He who is love is your love in a world of self-seeking. Indeed, He who is *the resurrection and the life* is now your very own Christian Life.

As you humbly make your life available to the Lord Jesus, who came *to seek and to save that which is lost (Luke19:10),* you now can also trust Him to seek and to save lost souls through you! Life becomes truly exciting when believers discover they are a channel of His life to other people.

Remember—though Jesus has returned to Heaven—He has certainly not removed Himself from you. When leaving His disciples on earth, He told them:

*After a little while the world will behold Me no more; but you will behold Me; because I live, you shall live also. In that day you shall know that **I am in My Father, and you in Me, and I in you** (John 14:19-20).*

Now you may ask, "How can all the resources that God has given me in Christ become real and practical in my life?" That's a good question. It recognizes the wide chasm between a faith that is mental and a faith that is experiential. The question also implies your deep desire for a faith that functions. The simple answer is that the triumphant life of Christ is released through the believer in response to thanks-giving. True faith always says, "Thank You."

For instance, the very best way you can express your saving faith in Christ is to thank Him that your sins have been forgiven. Now, you can also thank Him for the fact that He will become to you exactly what you need at the time you need it. *Without faith, it is impossible to please Him* [God] *(Hebrews 11:6).* As you desire to please Him, live your life of faith with constant thankfulness to the Lord Jesus for His sufficiency in all things.

When Peter wrote to Christians who because of their loyalty to the Lord Jesus Christ were suffering persecution, he exhorted: *Sanctify* [set apart; magnify; give full reign to] *Christ as Lord in your hearts . . . (1 Peter 3:15).* Therein lies God's open secret of how to cope when facing persecution for your faith. Be sure that Jesus is Lord of your life.

131

You may remember that one of the names of God in the Old Testament is Adonai. Adonai means Lord in the sense of His being my Master. It is this concept of *Lord God* as my Master that Peter used when he admonished believers by saying: *sanctify Christ as Lord in your hearts*.

As the Lord Jesus is master of your life you will enjoy His constant fellowship. Only then will you be truly free to trust Him with the daily demands and opportunities of your life. As the hymn writer, George Matheson, wrote:

> Make me a captive, Lord,
> And then I shall be free;
> Force me to render up my sword,
> And I shall conqueror be.

Contrary to the popular idea of freedom, real freedom is not found in my having the right to do what I want. Rather it is found in my having the power to do what I ought! Remember the words of the Apostle Paul who said: *I can do all things through Christ who strengthens me (Philippians 4:13 NKJ)*.

During the revival in Northern Ireland back in 1859, thousands of people came to Christ. Those converts expressed their own personal and serious commitment to Christ by signing a 'Commitment of Faith.' At that time, so many people had such a life-changing experience of the Risen Lord that the moral atmosphere of the country was literally transformed.

Although there is nothing meritorious in signing

such a document, perhaps at this time it would be helpful for you too, to confirm your own response to God by signing this document on the following pages.

> *Now the God of peace, that brought again from the dead our Lord Jesus, that great Shepherd of the sheep, through the blood of the everlasting covenant, make you perfect in every good work to do his will, working in you that which is well pleasing in his sight, through Jesus Christ; to whom be glory for ever and ever. Amen (Hebrews 13:20-21 KJ).*

A Letter from Hungary

"*Thank you so much for sending me the Holy Bible together with the book by Richard A. Bennet:* Your Quest for God.

"*I finished the book and checked every reference with the Bible.*

"Your Quest for God *helped me very much to clarify* what I *should believe and why I should believe. Now I am a Believer and, with the help of this book, I have made my life-time commitment of faith.*"

– *Report translated and submitted by Trans World Radio*

Now to help you make your own

Commitment of Faith
Scriptures are recorded
on Pages 136 and 137.

My Commitment of Faith

I take God the Father to be my God
You turned to God from idols to serve a living and true God.
(1 Thessalonians 1:9)

I take Jesus Christ to be my Lord and Savior
He (Jesus) *is the one whom God exalted to His right hand as a*
Prince and a Savior, to grant repentance . . . and forgiveness of sins.
(Acts 5:31)

I take the Holy Spirit to Fill me with the Love of God
Because the love of God has been poured out within our hearts
through the Holy Spirit who was given to us.
(Romans 5:5)

I take the Word of God to be my Rule
All scripture is inspired by God and is profitable for teaching, for
reproof, for correction, for training in righteousness; that the man of
God may be adequate, equipped for every good work.
(2 Timothy 3:16,17)

I take the People of God to be my People
Your people shall be my people, and your God my God.
(Ruth 1:16)

I dedicate myself wholly to the Lord

For not one of us lives for himself, and not one dies for himself; for if we live, we live for the Lord, or if we die, we die for the Lord; therefore whether we live or die, we are the Lord's.
(Romans 14:7,8)

And I do this Deliberately

Choose for yourselves today whom you will serve . . . but as for me and my house, we will serve the Lord.
(Joshua 24:15)

And Sincerely

In holiness and godly sincerity, not in fleshly wisdom but in the grace of God, we have conducted ourselves in the world.
(2 Corinthians 1:12)

And Freely

Thy people will volunteer freely in the day of Thy power. . . .
(Psalm 110:3)

And For Ever

Who shall separate us from the love of Christ? Shall tribulation, or distress, or persecution, or famine, or nakedness, or peril, or sword?
(Romans 8:35)

Signed: _____

Date: _____

**Now you are
encouraged to read
the author's sequel
to this book:**

*Food
for
Faith*

**Just as a person could be fascinated with recipes in
a cookbook and yet die of starvation, so one can be
fascinated with biblical 'recipes' for successful living and
still remain spiritually malnourished!**

**Food for Faith is a biblical manual written to help you
digest the Word of God from your hand—to your head—to
your heart.**

Published by
Cross Currents International Ministries
P.O. Box 1058
Lynden, WA 98264

www.ccim-media.com/resources